About the Author

Few people are as well
qualified to offer aid to
those who raise and care
for house plants as is the
author of this book.

T. H. Everett, presently
Senior Horticulture Spe-
cialist of the New York
Botanical Garden, devel-
oped and maintained one of
the largest and best-known
collections of living plants
in America. As an author
and lecturer, a teacher of
gardening and a gardening
columnist, he has been
known by thousands of
home gardeners for
many years.

S0-DNN-470

Fawcett Gold Medal Books by T. H. Everett:

HOW TO GROW BEAUTIFUL HOUSE PLANTS

101 FLOWERING HOUSE PLANTS ANYONE CAN GROW

101
Flowering
House Plants
Anyone
Can Grow

T. H. EVERETT

A FAWCETT GOLD MEDAL BOOK

Fawcett Publications, Inc., Greenwich, Conn.

Cover and Page 1 Photos: Kaffir Lily

101 FLOWERING HOUSE PLANTS ANYONE CAN GROW

Unless otherwise credited, photographs in this book are by
T. H. Everett.

Printed in the United States of America

First printing June 1975

1 2 3 4 5 6 7 8 9 10

Contents

Introduction

The urge to grow house plants is strong and innate. It has been my fortune to travel widely, to observe closely the horticultural efforts of peoples, and wherever I have traveled, I found folks cherishing plants in containers in and around their homes. In such countries as Germany, Holland, and Switzerland, windows fronting the street are customarily gay with begonias, fuchsias, geraniums, and other flowering sorts in marvelous bloom. The inhabitants of Hong Kong must be among the world's most skilled growers of plants in containers; not only in homes and gardens of the affluent, but also in the meanest parts, one finds near doorways, in windows, and on balconies, plants thriving in tin cans and other improvised containers. They are displayed at the sterns of Chinese junks, alongside cages of chickens.

The houseboat dwellers along the klongs of Bangkok are enthusiastic growers of potted plants. Some raise plants for sale; their vessels are their nurseries as well as their homes. I have seen house plants treasured by the people of the high valleys of Kashmir, by the citizens of Tegucigalpa, Honduras, and by Indians high in the Andes. In Communist countries, house plants find favor as they do elsewhere. Wherever I have traveled I have observed the need of people to grow plants in their homes.

In America the vogue for house plants constantly expands, and so does the number of sorts available. City apartment dwellers are as enthusiastic as suburbanites and country people. A considerable trade has developed to serve their needs. Garden centers, general nurseries, florists, and the modern equivalents of dimestores are all possible sources of plants. Even wider selections, including sorts interesting and new,

7

are available from specialist house-plant greenhouses which offer small plants for sale by mail. A list of such sources is given at the end of this book.

In recent years the technique of substituting fluorescent light for sunlight has come up, and a whole new generation of indoor light gardeners pursues this hobby. American homes, covering a vast geographical range, are lighted, heated, and cooled to varying degrees and by various methods, affording a tremendous variety of environments for plants. While there is probably no one home in which all the plants presented in this book can be grown, surely a goodly number of sorts, chosen with thought to prevailing conditions, can be successfully brought to flower in any house or apartment. One dividend of the much-discussed energy shortage is—if it results in lower temperatures maintained at nights in American homes—that many house plants will be healthier and will bloom more profusely.

T. H. EVERETT

How to Grow and Care for House Plants

In selecting flowering plants, consider what you want of them and the environments you can offer. A few presented in this book are in the gift-plant category: one-shot decoratives generally acquired in bloom and, having finished flowering, not suitable for maintaining indoors. Examples are hyacinths, primroses, and Easter lilies. I include such sorts because to keep them attractive as long as possible, one must know something of their needs, and, if properly cared for, most can be planted outdoors with every expectation that they will bloom again there.

The majority of the plants treated in this book will, if given proper care in matters such as watering, fertilizing, and repotting when needed, live indefinitely, bloom regularly, and can be propagated by simple means. A few are annuals, easily raised and grown from seeds. But no plant thrives unless conditions are reasonably suitable to its particular needs. Plants are far more sensitive than are animals or man to such factors as light, atmospheric humidity, and temperature. With some, you must respect dormant or resting seasons by keeping them dry—or at least drier than at other times— and usually cooler.

Light. Most, but not all, blooming house plants require more light than the majority of sorts grown for their foliage only. This means that if natural light is relied upon, as from a window, say, its intensity must be greater than would satisfy many foliage plants. But inadequate natural light can, to a considerable extent, be compensated for by supplementing it with, or in some cases entirely substituting for it, artificial light.

Even the brightest artificial illumination can not approach the intensity of a sunny day. But it can increase the intensity of light on dull days, improve that of locations poorly illuminated by daylight, and lengthen the day if you keep lights on 14 to 16 hours out of each 24. Plants so lighted are able to soak up, as it were, as much energy (needed for growth and other life processes) over the longer periods as they would under shorter exposures to natural light.

When natural light is inadequate, it helps to make use of that from ordinary incandescent bulbs, but because these give off heat, plants should not be placed too close to them. A better, much less expensive method is to use fluorescent bulbs. Light from these, sometimes supplemented with a small amount of incandescent light, is invariably the choice of those who grow plants with only artificial illumination.

Humidity. Atmospheric humidity is a factor of prime importance. Dry air causes excessive water loss from foliage and other above-ground parts. If this is more than the roots can replace, the plant endeavors to bring about a balance by dropping leaves and by growing fewer and smaller new leaves. Keeping the soil constantly moist is obviously helpful in counteracting this, but only to a point. If it is kept so wet that air is denied entry, the roots are likely to rot, with the result that the plant's ability to absorb water is further reduced. Exposure to drafts greatly increases water loss.

Terrariums—tanks of glass or plastic much like aquariums with covered tops—surround plants with a moister atmosphere than that of the room in which they stand. Results are still better if the terrarium is illuminated from the outside by fluorescent lights.

Humidity in indoor light gardens can be raised by enclosing or partly enclosing them with curtains of polyethylene plastic. There are other ways of raising humidity. One is to arrange plants in groups so that the water vapor given off by them raises the humidity in their immediate vicinity. Another is to stand pots in broad, shallow trays filled with sand, gravel, moss, or similar material kept constantly moist. Misting foliage a few times a day gives helpful but transient relief. Covering plants at night with plastic bags assures regular periods of higher humidity. Since indoor humidity drops precipitously as temperatures rise, growing plants in as cool environments as are reasonably practicable for their kinds is of great importance. Kinds of plants vary greatly in their tolerances. Those from desert and semidesert regions, most with thick, fleshy stems or leaves, like dry air; indeed, these are likely to be harmed by excessive humidity. Plants from humid habitats are far more sensitive.

Temperatures. Temperatures present from fall to spring, especially at night, are far more critical than summer levels. All the plants we consider in this book survive, and most revel, in normal summer temperatures. True, a few—tuberous begonias, fuchsias, and the campanula which New Englanders call star-of-Bethlehem—are uncomfortable when nights as well as days are very hot. In regions of torrid summers, these must be eliminated as possibilities as house plants, or be accommodated in partially shaded locations which are as cool as possible. Unfortunately, air conditioning rarely provides relief; even when it is in use, night temperatures are rarely reduced into the 60s, which most cool-temperature plants prefer. Worse, it dries the air.

Temperatures suggested throughout this book are based on those considered ideal minimums on winter nights. Up to 5° F. lower or higher usually works no great harm, but greater discrepancies can. Daytime levels may always exceed those maintained at night by 5 to 15° F.

Temperatures are likely to vary in different parts of a room. Near a window, they are often much lower, especially during cold weather, than those only a few feet away. Test the temperatures *near* the plants instead of going by those recorded by a thermometer in another location. To circumvent damage on very cold nights, it may be necessary to move the plants, to pull down shades, or to put several thicknesses of paper between the glass and the plants.

Soils. Soils for house plants should be porous to permit water to pass through them freely. If they won't do this, water fills the pores between the particles, air is driven out, and the roots rot. Some plants demand more porous soils than others. Porosity is achieved by mixing in nonorganic materials such as coarse sand, grit, perlite, or crushed brick. These are added to soil in varying amounts, depending upon whether the topsoil is sandy, loamy, or clayey, and according to the needs of different sorts of plants. For example, cactuses and other succulents need more porous soil than do geraniums.

In addition to topsoil and nonorganic additives, more organic matter is usually needed, and again the proportions of this are adjusted to the preferences of the particular kind of plant. In general, plants of woodland habitats which need shade from strong sun—such as African violets and gloxinias —also need more organic matter than other plants. The usual organic materials used are good semidecayed compost, leaf mold, and peat moss. Because organic matter gradually decays, eventually achieves a muddy texture, and may become sour, it is helpful to mix some crushed charcoal with soils that contain much of it.

Fertility is best assured by adding organic fertilizers. Dried cow manure, used at up to about 1/10 part by bulk of the total mix, and bonemeal, used at up to 2 heaped tablespoonfuls to each pint, are most appropriate and convenient. Both are sold by garden centers and other dealers.

Most plants do best in slightly acid soil, and some, especially those that revel in high percentages of organic matter, definitely need acid conditions; if the topsoil is not acid, use acid peat moss as the organic material. Some few plants need alkaline soil and benefit from crushed limestone or crushed clam or oyster shells in the mix.

Preferred mixes are sold and are convenient. Often they contain too little soil in proportion to organic matter, except for woodlander plants that prefer such mixes. For other plants, add some topsoil and some nonorganic material for porosity.

Watering. Many plants are killed by overwatering, and the growth of others is limited by watering too little. Actually what matters is the degree of moistness at which the soil is maintained. Except when plants are dormant, the soil must never be quite dry, but in most cases it should approach dryness before being given a soaking.

More frequent watering is needed when (1) the plant is large in comparison to the size of the pot, and has much foliage; (2) the container is well filled with healthy roots; (3) the plant is in active growth; (4) the temperature is fairly high; (5) atmospheric humidity tends to be low; (6) weather is bright and sunny; (7) plant is exposed to moving air (as when it stands in a partly opened window or outdoors in summer).

Fertilizing. Many beginners place too much reliance on fertilizers. They help only plants that are otherwise healthy but are in need of nutrients. Don't fertilize plants that are newly potted, dormant, or beginning to go dormant, or when the soil is quite dry. Many commercial fertilizers are available in powder, pill, and liquid forms. In general, I favor the liquids, and I believe in adding up to twice as much water as is recommended by the manufacturer. Weak and often is better.

Bugs and Blights. Except for a few, mostly easy to control, bugs and blights are not serious on house plants. Examine your specimens frequently and closely (under the leaves as well as above), and if troubles develop, take prompt remedial action.

Aphids or plant lice are slow-moving, green, reddish, or blackish, soft-bodied insects that congregate on succulent plant parts, usually on the younger stems and leaves. They are easily killed by spraying them with or dipping them in a contact insecticide such as malathion or pyrethrum.

Crown rot diseases result in the centers of the plants rotting. They are usually associated with poor soil drainage and excessive watering. Correct the causes. Cut out decayed parts. Dust with sulphur.

Damping-off disease causes the death of young seedlings. The stems collapse near the soil line. It is most damaging to seedlings that are thin and excessively long as a result of too high temperatures and insufficient light. It is less likely to attack seedlings raised in vermiculite, perlite, or milled sphagnum moss than those grown in soil. If it occurs, dust with powdered sulphur and transplant to new soil as soon as possible. Avoid keeping the soil or plants too wet.

Leaf spot diseases, generally result in small yellow or brown spots on the foliage. They are caused by fungi, bacteria, and, more rarely, viruses. Pick off affected leaves. Keep the plants widely spaced. Don't wet their foliage.

Mites are nearly transparent creatures, practically invisible to the naked eye. They cause distortion and hardening of infested foliage. Control of some sorts can be had by spraying with kelthane or applying dusting sulphur. More difficult kinds may be eliminated by submerging the plant for 15 minutes in water accurately maintained at 110° F.

Powdery mildew disease and gray mold blight produce yellowish-gray to whitish, moldy, sometimes water-soaked areas on leaves and stems. Avoid this by arranging for good air circulation. If either develops spray with karathane or benlate or dust with sulphur.

Red spider mites, scarcely seeable yellowish to reddish creatures that congregate chiefly on the undersides of leaves, spin fine webs there and result in the foliage becoming grayish- or silvery-speckled; these are most numerous where the air is hot and dry. Spraying with, or dipping the plants in, a solution of kelthane gives control.

Scale insects are brown to nearly black roundish lumps that develop on stems and leaves; when they reach observable size, they don't move. They can be picked off with a fingernail or similar instrument. The best way to remove them is to dip a sponge or soft toothbrush in malathion or sevin insecticide and gently rub or scrub the infested parts. Then wash them clean with water.

Whiteflies are tiny, white, mothlike insects that rise in small clouds when an infested plant is disturbed. They are difficult to control. The most reliable method is to spray (on dull days or at night when the creatures are sluggish) with malathion and repeat this weekly for a month to six weeks.

Mealybugs look somewhat like small tufts of white cotton. Control is as for scale insects, but less rubbing is needed.

About Plant Names and Families

A few words about the array of plant names and plant families to be found even in a modest grower's handbook like this.

Amateur gardeners are generally interested in plant family relationships but are not always clear about what a plant family is. Roughly, botany divides all the known plants in the world into families, all the families into *genera* (that's the plural of *genus*) and each genus consists of *species* (*species* is both singular and plural). Some genera comprise one species each, but most include more.

Every plant in this book has been classified by the botanists. Some have been reclassified because the botanists have found new evidence or have re-evaluated their earlier conclusions. Therefore, every plant described here has its botanical name in the rather odd Latin form which is still the international language of the life sciences.

Take *Rhoeo spathacea*. *Rhoeo* tells you what genus the plant belongs to; *spathacea* tells you which species it is of that genus. (Genus name first; Jones Tom instead of Tom Jones.) If you are a botanist you have memorized the families and genera, so you know that *Rhoeo* belongs to the spiderwort family, for which the Latin name is *Commelinaceae*. Botanists commonly use either the Latin or English name for a plant family.

What are species, genera, and families? First, a species (like *Rhoeo spathacea*) is a kind of plant that perpetuates itself in the wild without human assistance—a stubborn kind, insistent on being itself; and all the individual plants of this kind are enough alike so that they might be the offspring of one parent plant. (Which, of course, they are not.) A genus consists of one or more species that resemble each other more than they do species of other genera. These resemblances are anatomical, not surface ones. Species of a genus may *look* like each other or, on brief acquaintance, not like each other at all. Finally, plant families consist of a number of genera that are believed to be more closely related to each

14

other than to genera of other families. It sometimes happens that a family consists of one genus.

Species are frequently divided into natural and man-raised *varieties,* the man-raised varieties sometimes being called *cultivars.* To the gardener the cultivars are usually the pets of enthusiasts devoted to growing something extreme or beautiful in the way of color or form. Left to themselves in the wild, cultivars usually disappear, their seed-raised offspring reverting to ancestral type. Horticultural varieties are usually named not by botanists but by nurserymen and various other subscientific individuals and groups.

All this information can be helpful to the gardener, but you can have great pleasure from growing plants without ever getting it all straight.

Finally, the common names of plants. These are the names the best-known plants are known and loved by; daisy, pansy, forget-me-not, busy lizzie, black-eyed susan, passionflower, sweet William, etc. In the case of *Rhoeo spathacea,* it has several common names; moses-in-a-cradle, moses-in-a-boat, and oyster plant.

Some plants have no common names; often this is because they are not common plants. And we may be sure that somewhere, say in the depths of the Amazonian forest, there are plants no man has seen—no explorer, no botanist, no Indian —and these plants have no names at all, which does not bother them in the least.

Each caption number in the picture sections refers to
the descriptive entry of the same number.

Numbers 1–35 *are small- to moderate-sized plants for permanent cultivation indoors. A few can be grown into large specimens, if one wishes.*

1. African Violet

1 🌲 African violets (*Saintpaulia*) aren't relatives of true violets but achimenes, flame violets, and gloxinias. They belong in the gesneria family. The first species, *S. ionantha,* was discovered not far from Mount Kilimanjaro in East Africa in 1892, but the initial third of the 20th century had passed before they became popular—at first, only with gardeners with greenhouses. It was found they could be grown as well in homes as greenhouses, and, as a result of spontaneous sporting and later hybridizing, new varieties, eventually in a vast array of sizes, forms, and colors, became available. Thus the floodgates leading to their unprecedented popularity opened. African violets largely led the escape from our dull reliance upon a few house plants such as aspidistras, Boston ferns, and palms to the present national passion for growing a gorgeous and wonderful variety of living plants indoors. African violets are evergreen, stemless or short-stemmed perennials, with rosettes of long-stalked, fleshy, hairy, rounded to more or less heart-shaped, often slightly scalloped or

toothed leaves. The violetlike flowers, several on branched stems, are white, pink, lavender, blue, purple, violet, or bicolored. There are double and single-flowered kinds and many other variants.

How to grow. Their requirements are simple. They grow as well in indoor light gardens as in windows. (Some people say better.) Room specimens, if away from windows, benefit from being near a lamp if not too close to the heat. Propagation is easy by division, or by cuttings set in sand, perlite, vermiculite, or water, or by seeds. Pot in a loose soil mix containing abundant organic matter and no lime. Keep this pleasantly moist, not saturated. Try to keep 50% atmospheric humidity, temperatures in the 65 to 75° F. range. Water with tepid water. Don't wet foliage.

2 ❧ The apostle plant, or 12-apostles (*Neomarica northiana,* formerly *Marica northiana*), is irislike. It has fans of foliage of which it is said that 12 leaves develop before one withers; hence the popular names. Actually, unless the environment is favorable, the fans may never attain a dozen leaves. Native of Brazil and a member of the iris family, this has pointed, sword-shaped leaves about 1½ feet long by an inch or more wide and overlapping at their bases. They arise from a short rhizome. The flower stalks exceed the leaves. Their upturned, fragrant blooms, which last for one day only, provide a succession. They are 3 to 4 inches wide and have 3 wide-spreading pure white outer petals and 3 smaller violet-colored inner ones. After the flowers fade, small plantlets usually develop in their places. Also cultivated, *N. gracilis* of Brazil has foliage fans of 6 to 9 leaves and 2 inch-wide white flowers with brown markings.

How to grow. Apostle plants need surprisingly little care. Good light, either full sun or with a little protection from the most intense rays if needed. Humidity should be 30% or better. Provide 55 to 60° F. on winter nights with an increase to about 70° F. by day, with higher temperatures in summer. Pot any time, perferably in spring, in porous, nourishing soil containing a moderate amount of organic matter. Mix in bonemeal at the rate of two heaped teaspoonfuls to the pint. Keep soil moderately moist. Give well-rooted specimens dilute liquid fertilizer twice a month, spring to fall. For best results, limit each plant to one fan of leaves. Propagation is by division and by bending down flower stems bearing plantlets and pinning the latter to soil into which they will root, after which they can be severed and potted separately.

3 ❧ Angel-wing begonias are a group of varieties without thick surface rhizomes or underground tubers. They have canelike stems with distantly-spaced, swollen joints, and leaves shaped like the conventional portrayals of the wings of angels. They are pointed-elliptic and lopsided, with one basal lobe carried much beyond the point where the leafstalk joins the blade. The margins of the leaves are smooth and wavy or shallowly angled or toothed. The flowers are pink, red, or white. These plants are members of the begonia family. Angel-wing begonias include *Begonia coccinea* of Brazil and hybrids of it often identified by nonbotanical names such as "Lucerna," "President Carnot," and "Veitch's Carmine." They are 3 to 4 feet or more tall but bloom freely and nearly continuously when much smaller. Their stems branch above. The leaves hang more or less vertically, are 3 to 6 inches long, and sometimes are silvery-spotted. The flowers are in pendant fork-branched clusters of considerable size from the leaf axils. Male blooms have 2 large and 2 small petals; females have petals with behind them a showy, 3-winged ovary.

How to grow. Among the easiest of the vast begonia clan to manage. Needs 55 to 60° F. on winter nights with a daytime rise up to 75° F., humidity of 50% or better, ideally. Will survive with less. Needs bright, diffuse light; a window shaded from middle-of-the-day summer sun is satisfactory. Pot in coarse soil, 2/5 organic matter by bulk, the remainder equal parts on fertile topsoil and coarse sand, grit, or perlite. Add some broken charcoal; use bonemeal at the rate of a heaped teaspoonful to the pint. Keep soil moist, not saturated. Give well-rooted specimens regular applications of dilute liquid fertilizer. Prune to shape and size and repot in spring. Cuttings root readily if planted in sand, perlite, or vermiculite in a humid atmosphere.

4 ❧ The "Iron Cross" begonia (*Begonia masoniana*) was named botanically to honor the English horticulturist Maurice Mason, who in 1952 introduced this fine plant to his native land from Singapore where he had discovered it growing in the botanical garden. At first it was thought to be of hybrid origin, but because it breeds true to type from seeds, it is now considered to be a natural species. However, no one knows where it grows as a wildling. It probably is native of Malaya or Indochina. Its slightly gray-green leaves have a dark purple-brown pattern in shape strongly reminiscent of the Iron Cross, the German war medal. The leaves are heart-

4. Iron Cross Begonia

shaped, have blades up to about 7 inches long by 5 inches wide, upper surfaces thickly clothed with tiny fleshy pimples. Although its sprays of flowers are less showy than those of many begonias, they are dainty and interesting. Individual blooms are small, greenish-white with maroon bristles on their outsides.

How to grow. Needs 60° F. or above, humidity not below 50%. Does well in a terrarium. Good examples often grown in indoor light gardens. Needs coarse, loose soil with about equal amounts good topsoil, organic matter, and coarse sand or perlite, some dried manure and bonemeal. Pack soil moderately firmly. Keep the soil evenly moist, not saturated. Mist foliage daily. Considerable shade is tolerated; enough to mitigate the harmful effects of strong sun is necessary. Propagate by division in spring or by seeds.

5 ❦ Rex begonias (*Begonia rex-cultorum*) come in many entrancing varieties some with identifying names such as "Merry Christmas," "Queen Wilhelmina," and "Salamander," others unnamed seedlings. They are complex hybrids between several native species of warmer parts of the Himalayan region. Although grown chiefly for the splendor of their foliage, which comes in great variety of patterns and combinations of greens, silvers, pinks, bronzes, and reds, these have also quite

5. Rex Begonia

lovely blooms. The leaves are hairy, prevailingly in lopsided heart shapes, with or without jagged margins. There are male and female flowers, both on the same plant. Conspicuously winged ovaries at back of the spreading petals identify females. In color the blooms vary from pink to white according to variety. These plants are members of the begonia family.

How to grow. A little more tricky to manage than many begonias. Need 60° F., humidity at least 50%, and shade from direct sun. Excellent terrarium plants. In locations not too arid or drafty, they can be grown in open rooms. Need coarse soil with liberal amounts of rich organic matter. It may contain ⅓ by bulk of perlite or coarse sand, a generous dash of dried cow or sheep manure, and bonemeal. Have pots well drained. Winter is a season of partial or complete rest for rex begonias. Then they tend to look shabby; soil must be kept dryish. In spring repot, resume watering. Keep soil moist, never soggy, until late fall. Poor soil drainage and excessive wetness spell death. In summer at 2-week intervals give dilute liquid fertilizer to well-rooted specimens. Mist foliage on sunny days. Rex begonias are increased by division in spring and by leaf cuttings any time. The latter may be wedge-shaped portions of leaves or whole leaves with veins slit in several places laid flat on a mixture of peat moss and sand and pinned or weighted down. Needs a very humid atmosphere, shade from direct sun; temperature of 70° F. or higher is best.

6 🌿 Wax begonias (*Begonia semperflorens*) are horticultural varieties of a Brazilian species. They have slender, succulent stems and somewhat fleshy, usually green or bronze-red foliage. Leaves are broadly oval to nearly round, 2 to 4 inches long. Profuse smallish blooms in white, pink, or red, usually single. There are sorts with lovely double, rosebudlike flowers and some, called calla-lily begonias, in which the younger leaves are predominantly or entirely pure white, the smallest ones remindful of the flowers of calla lilies. These last are, except where summers are cool, generally more difficult to grow than other sorts. Wax begonias are about the best-known members of the begonia family, familiar as good-natured window plants, and candidates for indoor light gardens. If denied maximum sunlight they tend to go leggy, even

6. Wax Begonia

straggly. This can be partly countered by judicious pruning and by repropagating fairly frequently. This last is easily done. For indoor cultivation, select naturally compact varieties.

How to grow. Propagate from cuttings or seeds. Both are easy. Plant cuttings in sand, perlite, vermiculite, or even water at about 70° F. Sow the minute seeds on the surface of very fine soil or milled sphagnum moss without covering. Germinate them at about 70° F. Transplant seedlings an inch apart as soon as they are big enough to handle. Best soil is porous, fair proportion of organic matter; keep it moderately moist, let it go fairly dry between waterings. Fertilize lightly; excess nitrogen encourages rank growth. Ordinary house temperatures and humidities suit. Keep window plants in full sun. Pinch tips out of the shoots occasionally to induce bushiness. Repot any time in spring or summer.

7. Bird-of-Paradise Flower

7 🌿 Bird-of-paradise flower (*Strelitzia reginae*) is a robust evergreen perennial of the banana family. *"Reginae,"* meaning "of the queen," honors Queen Charlotte, wife of George III.

The remarkably shaped and strikingly colored big blue and gold flowers (really groups of flowers with attendant leafy bracts) of this species are commonly sold as cut flowers. They can be had on specimens at home if the right care is afforded them but only strong, robust plants are likely to bloom satisfactorily. The bird-of-paradise flower has no obvious stem or trunk. Its long-stalked leathery leaves have pointed, paddle-shaped blades 9 inches to 1½ feet in length and 4 to 6 inches broad. As long or nearly as long as the leaves, the stout flower stalks are topped by a head of flowers set in a long, pointed, boat-shaped bract, the "beak" of the "bird," from out of which the 3- to 4-inch-high floral parts, royal blue and rich golden yellow, stand erectly to form the crest on the head of the "bird."

How to grow. You may start with seeds, easy to germinate in sandy soil at 60 to 70° F., and wait 5 years or more to flowering, or begin with an established plant of blooming size or smaller. Needs well-lighted window or sunroom, winter temperature 55 to 60° F., at night, 70° F. by day, summer temperatures higher. Humidity should be at least 30%, preferably quite a bit higher. Water generously spring to fall, less often in winter. If pot is full of roots, give dilute liquid fertilizer every 2 weeks spring to fall. Soil: should be loamy, not too sandy, not too clayey, not too much organic matter. Mix equal parts of fertile topsoil, organic matter, coarse sand, grit or perlite. Add to this 1/10 part by bulk dried cow manure, 2 heaped tablespoonfuls of bonemeal to each pint of mixture. Pack soil firmly. Until plants occupy containers 8 or 9 inches in diameter, repot every two years if growth warrants; repot large specimens at intervals of several years.

8. Blue Marguerite or Blue Daisy

8 ❧ The blue marguerite or blue daisy (*Felicia amelloides*) is a bushy, evergreen shrublet of South Africa frequently cultivated under the now obsolete name of *Agathaea coelestis*. It belongs in the daisy family and is a pleasing window plant that blooms nearly continuously, and is especially profuse in late fall. From 1 to 1½ feet or more in height, this has opposite, short-stalked, elliptic to oblong-egg-shaped, slightly aromatic leaves about an inch long, and toothless or scarcely toothed. The daisylike flower heads are solitary atop comparatively long, leafless stalks. From 1 to 1¼ inches in diameter, they have a bright yellow center or "eye" and many beautiful sky-blue rays commonly but mistakenly identified as petals. Each is, as are the smaller components that make up the "eye" or disk, in fact, a separate little flower called a floret. This is characteristic of the flower heads (usually called flowers) of plants of the daisy family.

How to grow. Sow seeds in porous soil at 60 to 65° F. in spring or late summer, or plant cuttings any time in sand, vermiculite, or perlite, 60 to 65° F. Transfer seedlings big enough to handle to individual small pots. Treat rooted cuttings the same. Use fairly sandy soil. Keep young plants in sun at 50 to 55° F. by night, up to 60° F. by day. When small pots are filled with roots, repot into pots 4 inches in diameter, eventually into pots a size bigger. Pots must be well drained. Use fertile, porous soil. Pack it moderately firmly; keep it evenly moist. Pinch tips out of shoots occasionally to promote branching.

9 ❧ Cattleyas (*Cattleya*) are the familiar florist's orchids, most popular for corsages. Their forebears came from tropical America; a plant from São Paulo, Brazil, bloomed in Liverpool in 1810; ten years later William Cattley, a London nurseryman, noted a strange plant used as packing around other plants in a shipment from Rio de Janeiro. He planted some of the packing and grew it to blooming stage. Cattleyas are named for him. Wild cattleyas perch on trees without taking nourishment from them. They have above-ground swollen parts, called pseudobulbs, from the tops of which sprout one to three strap-shaped leaves and, in season, flowers —mostly pinkish-lavender to purple; there are also white blooms and yellow ones. C. *bowringiana*, C. *labiata*, C. *mossiae* and C. *trianae* are species more likely to succeed as house plants than are the hybrids. Cattleyas belong in the orchid family.

How to grow. These need special conditions; terrariums and indoor light gardens are best. Humidity should be 50% at least, at 60° F. by night and in winter, 70° F. by day. Pot in osmunda fiber or bark chips sold for orchids; keep this moist—not dry, not saturated. Give dilute liquid fertilizer every 7 to 10 days to well-rooted, actively growing plants. Propagate by division.

10 ❧ The clamshell orchid (*Epidendrum cochleatum*) well deserves its popular name. The up-pointing lip of each flower suggests a tiny nearly black-purple clamshell which has a white base with radiating lines of purple. Hanging below it

10. Clamshell Orchid

are 5 slender, twisted, greenish-yellow sepals and petals which give to the entire bloom a squid- or octopus-like aspect. Flowers are produced mostly from late summer to fall. This plant belongs in the orchid family. Native from Florida to Mexico to Cuba and Brazil, this orchid forms clusters of bulblike stems (pseudobulbs). From the top of each of these grow 1 to 3 pointed, narrowly elliptic, leathery leaves, each 3 to 5 inches long, 1 to 2½ inches wide. The flower stalks each have several long-lasting blooms that open in succession. While less splendid than cattleyas, the clamshell is excellent for growing in terrariums, indoor light gardens, and even on windowsills in rooms where the air is not too arid.

How to grow. This orchid is an epiphyte. In the wild it perches on trees, rooting into crotches and bark crevices where there are accumulations of organic debris, taking no nourishment from the tree. Plant in fir bark chips, osmunda fiber, or one of the rooting mixes prepared for epiphytic orchids. Plant with the bottoms of the pseudobulbs level with the top of the rooting medium. Make the latter firm and keep it moderately moist. Grow in good light with some shade from strong summer sun. Try to keep humidity 50% or higher. Mist the foliage on bright days but not to the extent that water collects in the bases of the leaves. Winter temperature: 55 to 60° F. by night, up to 70° F. by day. At other seasons more warmth is OK. Fertilize well-rooted plants monthly from spring to fall. Increase it by careful division in spring.

11. Crossandra infundibuliformis

11 🌿 *Crossandra infundibuliformis* is a discouraging name yet the plant burdened with it is amazingly popular. A charming member of the acanthus family, in favorable environments it responds very well to pot culture indoors. Native of India, this is a subshrub or shrub, outdoors in the tropics 1 to 3 feet tall. As a house plant can be kept less than a foot high. It has lustrous, wavy, lance-shaped leaves 3 to 5 inches long and dense terminal spikes, up to 4 inches in length, of very beautiful, showy, salmon-orange flowers each about an inch across. The spikes open their blooms in succession from the base up and remain attractive for quite a long time. As the earlier ones pass out of bloom other spikes follow. A variety named "Mona Wallhed" has blackish-green foliage and salmon-pink flowers.

How to grow. Dryness is the enemy. If you can provide 50% humidity, as in a terrarium, in most indoor light gardens, and often in a window fitted with a tray filled with gravel kept moist, you should have little difficulty.

Plant it in a pot slightly small for the size of the plant, in fertile soil with generous organic matter. Keep this evenly moist, not saturated. Fertilize well-rooted plants every 14 days spring to fall. Needs good light, some shade from strong sun; 55 to 60° F. of a winter night, up to 75° F. by day. Pinch the tips out of the stems as is needed to encourage branching. Increase is easy by seeds and by cuttings planted in sand, perlite, or vermiculite in a humid, shaded place at 70° F.

26

12. Emerald Ripple

12 🌿 Emerald ripple (*Peperomia caperata*) is handsome of foliage, decorative in bloom. It belongs in the pepper family and so is related to the tropical vine that is the source of the condiment rather than of the peppers of the vegetable garden. A native of Brazil, like most peperomias this is a forest floor plant or occupies mossy footholds at the bases of trunks and sometimes crotches and crevices on the branches of trees. Small and densely-foliaged, this species has a short, branching stem and roundish heart-shaped slightly fleshy leaves with neatly corrugated surfaces. They are about 1½ inches in diameter, green with the bottoms of the valleys of the corrugations toned with chocolate-brown and their ridges often grayish. The individual flowers, too small to be readily identifiable, are crowded into slender, erect, pale greenish-white, smooth, cylindrical spikes. A variety named "Little Fantasy" is dwarfer and smaller in all its parts. A choice kind but more difficult to grow than the others is "Tricolor Ripple" (*P. caperata tricolor*). This has milky-green leaves with broad creamy-white margins. Their bases and along the veins are suffused with red.

How to grow. Good plants for terrariums, generally satisfactory in dish gardens; tolerant of rather low humidities but lusher in moist air. Ordinary house temperatures agree with them, and moderately shaded locations. Soil: mix one part each topsoil and coarse sand or perlite and 2 parts organic matter; add bonemeal, a heaped teaspoonful to a pint. Pack soil only moderately. Keep the soil fairly moist, let it dry a little between waterings. Propagation is quite simple by stem cuttings or leaf cuttings planted in sand, perlite, or vermiculite.

13 ❧ Episcias (*Episcia*) are in the same gesneria family as achimenes, African violets, and gloxinias, but they don't look much like any of the others. They are trailing or creeping plants from Central and South American forests. Blooms come in white, lilac, yellow, and red; the red sorts are called flame violets because they are related to African violets. Episcias have opposite, broadly elliptic to egg-shaped, generally hairy leaves, mostly 3 to 4 inches long and shallowly toothed. Their 5 petaled, tubular blooms, about an inch wide, have flat faces. The foliage of some sorts is marbled or otherwise variegated or toned with silvery-gray, white, pink, cream, brown, or red or with mixtures of these.

How to grow. Episcias look best in hanging baskets or planters that allow their foliage and blooms to cascade. Keep at 60° F., at least 30% humidity. Soil: coarse with plenty of organic matter, coarse sand or perlite, small pieces of charcoal to sweeten. Spring, early summer best for potting. Don't pack soil too firmly; keep evenly moist; occasionally put dilute liquid fertilizer on well-rooted plants. Propagation is easy by cuttings in sand, perlite, or vermiculite, or by pinning stems down onto soil, taking off young plants that develop from them.

14 ❧ Flamingo flowers, or tail flowers (*Anthurium*), are species and hybrids of tropical South American natives of the arum family. The name flamingo flower is restricted to sorts with inflorescences (generally called flowers) with showy red, pink, white, or variegated bracts (spathes). Flamingo flowers include very large plants, varieties of *Anthurium andraeanum*, with long-stalked, big-spathed inflorescences with a straight, spikelike "tail" (spadix) and less robust sorts with spathes only about 3 inches long and curly "tails." These last, *Anthurium scherzerianum* and its varieties, are the better house plants. As is characteristic of inflorescences of the arum family, their true flowers, tiny and as decorations inconsequential, are along the spadix. The spathe is showy and petallike. It doesn't, as do those of calla lilies and jack-in-the-pulpit, surround or enclose the spadix, but stands free from it.

How to grow. These need considerable warmth and humidity of 50% plus; do best in terrariums or such enclosures. Give good light but shade from strong direct sun except in depth of winter. Keep at 65° F. or above winter nights, higher other times. Soil: one part soil, 3 parts osmunda (peanut-to-walnut size) or tree fern fiber such as is used for orchids; add some coarse sand, grit, or perlite, and crushed charcoal.

Firm lightly; never let dry out. Give well-rooted plants dilute liquid fertilizer each 7 to 14 days. Increase by offsets or division in spring.

15 Flowering maples (*Abutilon*) owe their common name to the leaves of many sorts bearing a resemblance to those of maples not to any botanical relationship. These are old-fashioned favorites in the past called "parlor maples." They include species that inhabit various warm parts of the world and hybrids of same. Cultivated kinds are shrubby. Most grow erectly but some, notably *A. megapotamicum,* have trailing or pendulous stems and are suitable for hanging baskets. Flowering maples have alternate, long-stalked, lobed or toothed leaves, those of some varieties variegated with white or yellow, biggish, solitary, pendulous, bell-shaped blooms with a calyx that in some kinds is brightly colored, and 5 rounded petals. United into a column, the stamens hang like the clapper of a bell. In the main, the flower colors are muted rather than brilliant. Prevailing hues are white, yellow, tangerine, pink, and reddish. The petals are usually attractively veined with darker hues. These belong in the mallow family.

How to grow. Keep at 50 to 55° F. winter nights, up to 70° F. by day; humidity at least 40%. Cuttings from firm, not hard shoots root readily in vermiculite, sand, perlite, at 60 to 70° F. Soil: Don't fuss. Porous, fertile soil is good in well-drained pot. Water moderately year round; spring to fall dilute liquid fertilizer each 7 to 14 days. Prune to shape; repot old plants late winter or spring, young ones oftener if needed. Pinch out tips of shoots occasionally to induce branching.

16 Friendship plant is a pleasant name for the easy-to-grow bromeliad, *Billbergia nutans,* a member of the pineapple family. This species lends itself well to division and thus being shared by friends, who divide it again and give to other friends; hence the name. The majority of bromeliads, such as the Spanish moss so abundant in the Deep South, perch on trees without extracting nourishment from them. Others, including the pineapple, grow in the ground. In the forests of Brazil, Argentina, and Uruguay the friendship plant is found in both habitats. It forms tufts of mostly slender, erect, gracefully arching, sword-shaped leaves 8 inches to a foot long by ¼ inch or so wide. They are olive green, becoming reddish on plants in sunny locations. A variety with

16. Friendship Plant

spotted leaves is known, and also one with shorter, broader foliage than the typical kind. The flowers nod from the ends of stalks, each of which bears several. The lower parts of the stalk are erect. Above, they arch so completely that they become pendant and are decorated with pink bracts. The blooms have 3 rose-pink sepals and 3 backward-curved, blue-edged, jade green petals. They are borne throughout most of the year.

How to grow. Soil: mix osmunda fiber, orchid-mix bark chips, or coarse compost with smaller amount topsoil plus sand or perlite; since roots need drainage and air, provide a loose potting mix. Keep moist, not saturated. Dilute liquid fertilizer on well-rooted ones each 14 days. Ordinary house temperature, 30% humidity, shade from strong sun. Propagate by division.

17 ❧ Common geraniums of house plant fans and summer flowerbeds are not members of the botanical genus *Geranium*, although they belong to the geranium family. They are kinds of *Pelargonium*. Botanists' geraniums are represented in gardens by a few hardy herbaceous perennials with blue, red, pink, or white flowers. They die to the ground in winter. The geraniums that concern us here are not hardy in cold climates. Their foliage is evergreen. None has blue flowers. These are hybrid descendants of species native to South Africa. Because a horseshoe-shaped, darker zone can be seen on the leaves of most, they are called "zonal geraniums," or "fish geraniums" because of the subtle odor of their foliage when bruised. Their variety is vast. They range in size from miniatures smaller than a teacup to robust sorts that become 2 to 3 feet or more tall and wide. Their finely-hairy leaves are round to kidney-shaped, 1 to 5 inches across, have slightly scalloped or toothed margins. There are sorts with beautifully variegated foliage. In long-stalked clusters, the single or double blooms come in a wide range of reds and pinks as well as white. In bird's-egg varieties, the flowers are speckled with dots of another color.

How to grow. These need maximum sun, 50 to 55° F. winter nights, up to 70° F. by day, warmer in summer, 30 to 50% humidity. Propagate by cuttings in sand, perlite or vermiculite at 60 to 70° F. in humid atmosphere with shade from sun. Seeds do very well. Soil: well-drained, loamy, not too much organic matter or fertilizer, a little lime, packed firmly. Keep moist, not wet. Fertilize well-rooted ones moderately spring through fall. Pinch out shoots before they get leggy. Prune old ones to size and shape any time; spring is best.

18 ❧ Martha Washington or Lady Washington geraniums or pelargoniums, (*Pelargonium domesticum*) are of the geranium family. Like common geraniums they derive from species native to South Africa, but their forebears inhabited regions markedly drier in summer. From common geraniums, these differ in having much woodier stems, leaves without a darker zone, and bigger, asymmetrical, pansylike flowers that make one grand display in late winter or spring and disappear. Blooms vary from white through many shades of pink and red to black-crimson, usually with a few prominent darker blotches.

How to grow. These need full sun, cool conditions fall through spring. Starting with plant in bloom, water copiously while flowers last, then less and less often so plant dries between waterings, leaves yellow and some drop. In early June, quit watering, put plant outdoors with pot on its side. In late June, prune last year's shoots to an inch of bases; set pot upright, soak soil. Mist cut-back tops daily. When buds plump, before leaves develop, unpot plant, shake away old soil; repot in smaller pot with fertile, porous soil with some lime, packed firmly. Bury pot to rim in sun outdoors; resume normal watering. When roots fill pot, repot in larger one. Remove weak, crowded shoots; pinch tips of others at 6 inches. Repeat pinching to early January. Before frost, bring indoors to sunny window with 45 to 50° F. by night, not more than 60° F. by day. Put in bigger pot in January. Propagate by summer cuttings.

19. Gesneria

19 ❧ Gesnerias, except for the one we are about to consider, are uncommon in cultivation. Other plants, especially rechsteinerias, are often grown under their name. Ways of distinguishing between these two are given in our discussion of rechsteinerias. The naming genus of the gesneria family, *Gesneria* is native of tropical America. Our species, *G. cuneifolia,* hails from Puerto Rico and some other West Indian islands. It is a charming small sort with short branched stems and alternate, reverse-lance-shaped, toothed leaves 2 to 4½ inches long, green above, paler on their undersides. The inch-long, tubular flowers, in evidence almost throughout the year, are solitary on stalks that come from the leaf axils. They are clothed with minute white hairs. They come in 3 color forms. In one the flowers are red, in another yellow tipped with orange, those of the third are divided lengthwise into half red and half burnt-orange zones.

How to grow. Does best in terrarium or indoor light garden but can be raised in windows. Needs 65° F. or higher, 40% humidity or higher, at all times. Raising from seeds is best, but cuttings can be rooted. Best sowing, care and soil are as for rechsteinerias, which see. Gesneria has no rest season, unlike rechsteinerias. Shade from direct sun, never let soil go dry. Pots 3 to 4 inches across are ample.

20 ❧ *Haemanthus albiflos* of the amaryllis family seems not to have a common name, perhaps because it is not common. It is one of a group of African bulbous plants, some

2. Apostle Plant

3. Angel-wing Begonia

9. Orchid (Cattleya)

9. Orchid (Cattleya guatemalensis)

13. Episcia (Flame Violet)

14. Flamingo Flower

15. Flowering Maple

17. Geranium

18. Martha Washington Geranium

20. Haemanthus albiflos

20. Haemanthus albiflos (in Fruit)

23. Shrubby Monkey Flower

24. Moraea iridoides

with red flowers are called blood-lilies. But that would be inappropriate as a name for the plant we are discussing; it is not lilylike nor are its shaving-brush-like heads of bloom, each squatting on a collar of greenish bracts, sanguinary. They are white, with their many stamens tipped with golden yellow anthers. This species has bulbs up to tennis-ball size, from each of which sprout dull, fleshy, strap-shaped, evergreen leaves 6 to 9 inches long, fringed with hairs. The bulbs multiply freely to become crowded clusters. From among them rise stems 6 to 10 inches long each, bearing a flower head. The blooms are succeeded by long-lasting, attractive small berries, at first green, eventually bright red. An ideal house plant for collectors of rarities, this one is easy to manage.

How to grow. Plant bulbs with tip just buried in well-drained shallow pot of fertile, porous loamy soil. Keep in sunny window at 50 to 55° F. winter nights, up to 70° F. by day; dry atmosphere OK. Throughout year, water by soaking, then letting go nearly dry before soaking again. Give dilute liquid fertilizer every 14 days during active growth. Repot every 3 to 4 years, no oftener. Propagate by offset bulbs or sow seeds in sandy soil at 55 to 60° F. These take 3 years or more to reach blooming size.

21 ❧ The Kaffir-lily (*Clivia miniata*) of South Africa is not a true lily but belongs in the amaryllis family. Handsome in foliage as well as bloom, it has no real bulbs. Only rudimentary ones result from the thickening of the basal, overlapped parts of its evergreen, somewhat fleshy, 2-ranked, dark green, strap-shaped leaves. From the center of each strong fan of foliage emerges in late winter or spring an erect, stout, dark green stalk topped by a rounded cluster of up to about 20 flaring-trumpet-shaped, bright orange flowers with yellow throats. In the finest forms, the flowers are much bigger and fuller and have broader petals than in inferior ones. These are the ones to be sought.

How to grow. Begin with one fan of leaves and as large a mass of roots as can be conveniently taken with it. Pot this into well-drained container just big enough to accommodate root mass comfortably. Use coarse, fertile, porous soil; pack firmly, taking care not to damage brittle·roots. Keep newly-potted plants and established ones in a light place with some little shade from strong summer sun at winter temperature of 55 to 60° F. by night, up to 75° F. by day. Water moderately January—September, infrequently or scarcely at all rest of year. Fertilize well-rooted specimens from spring to fall. A summer vacation in a shady place outdoors or on a porch is beneficial. Propagation is by division and seeds. Seedlings take several years to reach blooming size. The Kaffir lily does best when roots are undisturbed and a little crowded, so don't re-pot frequently; at intervals of several years suffices. In intervening years prick away some surface soil each spring and replace with a rich mix.

22. Mexican Foxglove

22 🌿 The Mexican foxglove (*Tetranema mexicanum*) is sometimes offered under its synonymous name of *Allophyton mexicanum*. Whichever is used, one requires some little imagination to relate the plant to the true foxglove (*Digitalis*). Its manner of displaying its flowers and growth are quite different. Yet if the blooms are examined it will be seen that they bear some faint resemblance to those of foxgloves. Both plants belong to the figwort family. A charming miniature for terrariums and for window gardens where the atmosphere is not too arid, the Mexican foxglove is very easy to grow and gives a good account of itself by blooming almost continuously and most profusely through the summer. This is not a showy species but is quite charming when examined closely. An evergreen perennial, it has a short stem and foliage that spreads in more or less rosette fashion. The leaves are oblongish to narrowly reverse-egg-shaped, without stalks and of firm texture. They are 3 to 6 inches long. Lifted 4 to 6 inches above the foliage, the bracted flower stalks present loose sprays of nodding, ¼-inch-long trumpet-shaped blooms, rosy-violet with whitish lower lips.

How to grow. Grows so easily from seeds you rarely need

34

to propagate otherwise; can be divided in spring. Self-sown seeds commonly produce seedlings in soil or other nearby plants. Pot in ordinary fertile soil, well drained. Repot established plants each spring, small ones then and again in summer. Water moderately, so earth isn't always muddy. When pots are full of roots, give dilute liquid fertilizer each 14 days. In winter, 55 to 60° F. by night, 75° F. by day, warmer in other seasons.

23   Shrubby monkey flowers—which some botanists segregate from *Mimulus,* to which nonshrubby sorts belong, calling these *Diplacus*—are attractive natives of the Pacific Coast. They make very satisfactory house plants. They include two or three species and hybrids between them. Belonging to the figwort family, 1 to 3 feet tall, much branched and bushy, these bloom freely when quite small. They have pairs of glossy, narrow-oblong, often sticky leaves 1½ to 3 inches in length and plentifully produced tubular flowers 1 to 3 inches long and with 5 notched petals that form a decidedly 2-lipped face. They range from cream-colored through buff, yellow and apricot to orange, from soft pink to deep rich red.

How to grow. Start from seeds or cuttings. Plants from seeds may show variations in size or color of flowers or in growth habit. Cuttings give plants just like parent plant. Sow seeds in spring, sandy soil, 60 to 70° F.; plant cuttings in sand, perlite, or vermiculite, humid atmosphere, 60° F. or above. Pot seedlings, rooted cuttings, in small pots, sandy soil. Repot in 4-inch pots and successively bigger ones as roots fill pots. For later pottings, fertile soil that drains freely. When plants are 3 to 4 inches tall, pinch out tips; repeat this with branches that result when they are 5 to 6 inches long. Full sun except slight shade in high summer; 50 to 55° F. winter nights, 70° F. by day. Water moderately spring to fall, less in winter; give well-rooted ones dilute liquid fertilizer twice a month spring to fall. After main flush of bloom is over, prune part way back to encourage new shoots. Prune old plants to shape and size and repot in spring.

24   *Moraea iridioides* is the name of a very lovely iris-like native of South Africa. The similarity between it and *Iris* is acknowledged in its botanical name, the word *iridioides* deriving from irid, a group designation for any plant of the iris family, and the Greek *opsis,* similar to. No iris is native of the Southern Hemisphere. From short, tough, creeping rhizomes, *Moraea iridioides* sends crowded sheafs of fans of erect, dull green, narrowly sword-shaped, evergreen leaves 1½ to 2 feet tall. The wiry, sometimes branched flower stalks just exceed the foliage. Each bears 3 or 4 white flowers with yellow particles at the bases of the 3 broad, spreading petals. They are 3 inches or more wide. Several crops of bloom are displayed at intervals spring to fall.

How to grow. Most South African plants do best when cool in winter; 45 to 55° F. nights, 55 to 65° F. days; humidity 30% and up. Sunny location. When potting is needed (every few years), do it late winter or early spring. Ample drainage bottom of pot. Soil: mix equal parts fertile topsoil, organic matter, and coarse sand, grit or perlite; add 1/10 part by bulk dried cow manure, two heaped teaspoonfuls bonemeal to each pint. Pack firmly. Water freely spring to fall, less in winter but keep damp or leaf tips will brown and die back. Don't cut flowering stalks after blooming; next flowering develops from them. Propagate by division in spring.

25   Moses-in-the-cradle, moses-in-a-boat, or oyster plant (*Rhoeo spathacea*) is a popular, easy-to-grow species of the spiderwort family. Its flowers are apt to be overlooked—but not by the true house plant fan who delights in the amusing and quaint. Native of Mexico and the West Indies, *Rhoeo* consists of one species, *R. spathacea*. This has a short, thick, erect stem and symmetrically disposed spreading, inclined, and erect narrowly sword-shaped to nearly strap-shaped, fleshy leaves in

25. Moses-in-the-Cradle

a loose open rosette. The yare 6 inches to a foot in length, 1 to 3 inches wide, channeled in their lower parts and overlapping each other with their bases that hide the stem. In the typical sort the leaves are plain green above, purplish beneath. Variety *R. s. vittata* has yellow stripes running lengthwise down green leaves. The "cradle" or "boat," or if one prefers, the shells of the "oyster," are a pair of leafy large bracts that form an elliptic, protective cup around the cluster of small, frail, white blooms which are stand-ins for "Moses" or the "meat" of the oyster. Cradle and contents form an inflorescence, one or sometimes more of which develop close to the stem in each leaf axil.

How to grow. Easy house plant, does best 60° F. or higher, tolerates aridity, does better in moist air in good light with shade from full summer sun. Plant in broad, shallow, well-drained container in porous, rich soil kept moist. Fertilize at 14- to 28-day intervals. Cuttings root readily in sand, perlite, vermiculite.

26. Mosquito Plant

26 ❧ The mosquito plant (*Lopezia hirsuta* or *L. lineata*) is imaginatively named. Its dainty flowers suggest a swarm of pink mosquitos hovering near it. It neither draws nor discourages biting insects. Native of Mexico, the mosquito plant belongs in the evening primrose family. A somewhat sprawling or trailing subshrub, it has slender, much-branched stems that not infrequently root where they come into contact with the ground. The leaves, usually hairy and lance-shaped to heart-shaped, are ½ to 1½ inches long, the upper ones smaller than those below. Deep coral-pink to salmon-pink with the 2 narrowed petals generally paler than the others, the peculiarly shaped flowers are about ⅝ inch in diameter. They are borne in profusion and almost continuously from spring to fall. Although not exactly spectacular, this plant is an interesting, quite charming, easy-to-grow, sure bloomer. Similar *L. coronata* of Mexico is usually an annual that dies at the end of its first flowering season. Because of this, it is generally less satisfactory as a house plant than the other, and gardeners are sometimes disappointed when they acquire it rather than the perennial kind. However, it reproduces very easily from seeds, which it produces in some abundance.

How to grow. Perennial grows easily from seeds in sandy soil or from cuttings in humid air at 60 to 70° F. Shade cuttings until rooted. Pot seedlings or cuttings in small pots in sandy, fertile soil. Pinch tips of main stems and branches occasionally to promote branching. Put into bigger pots as growth requires. Does well with ordinary house conditions in sunny window or with part-day shade—also in indoor light gardens.

27 ❧ *Pentas lanceolata* is a free-flowering plant of the madder family with much to recommend it to the grower of indoor plants. It is easy to manage, grows rapidly, is readily controllable to size, and comes in a variety of flower colors. Native of tropical Africa and Arabia, it has much the appearance of its near-relatives bouvardias and ixoras. A branching, subshrubby plant 1 to 2 feet tall, this has pointed egg-shaped to lance-shaped, thinning, short-stalked leaves 1 to 4 inches or so long, from ½ to 2 inches wide. In crowded clusters of many, the early stalkless, up-facing blooms have slender inchlong corolla tubes and 5 petals that spread widely to form starlike faces. They are lavender-pink, pale pink, rose pink, red, or white.

How to grow. Start from seed spring or early summer at 60 to 70° F. in sandy soil; plants raised this way will show differences in height, compactness, and flower color. Cuttings reproduce parent plants exactly, rooted in sand, perlite, vermiculite, in humid air at 60 to 70° F., shaded from direct sun.

Pot seedlings or rooted cuttings singly in small pots of sandy soil. When 3 to 4 inches tall, pinch tips to aid branching; pinch off branches at 3 to 4 inches. When roots fill pots repot in 4-inch pots, later in 5- to 6-inch pots. Ordinary potting soil; pack firmly. Keep moderately moist. Fertilize well-rooted plants occasionally; stake and tie as needed; cut back straggly branches.

28 🌿 Poinsettias. It was 1833 before the first poinsettia was sent from its native Mexico to the United States. Its discoverer, Joel Poinsett of Charleston, South Carolina, was the first United States Minister to Mexico. Botanically *Euphorbia pulcherrima*, it belongs in the spurge family. Poinsettias are too familiar to require description. The hardy modern varieties that remain compact are an achievement of American plant breeders. The red, pink, or white organs that make the display are not petals but modified leaves called bracts. The flowers are little yellow organs centered in the bracts.

How to grow. Home-grown don't equal florist's poinsettias, but may be fun to raise. When display is over, trim off faded blooms, stop watering, store plant at 50 to 60° F. in dry place until May; then cut back to height of 9 inches. Pick such soil as you can easily from roots; repot in well-drained pot just big enough for roots. Use porous, fertile, loamy soil. Pot in sunny window, 60 to 70° F. Water moderately first, more freely as it grows. Limit shoots to 3. Repot when roots fill first pot. Pinch tips out of stems early August. When they branch, keep only a few strong shoots. Avoid drafts. To bloom, plants must have 12 hours uninterrupted darkness a night fall and winter.

29 🌿 *Setcraesea purpurea* was known as "Purple Heart" before it was described botanically in 1955. A Puerto Rican nurseryman traveling in Mexico in the early 1950s noticed the plant growing in a windowbox at the airport at Tampico. He took cuttings home, raised plants from them, and, be-

29. Setcreasea purpurea

cause, of the rapidity with which this species propagates, soon had an immense stock of young plants which he shipped to dimestores and the like in the U.S. In this lowly way "Purple Heart" made its debut. Related to the wandering jew and so a member of the spiderwort family, *Setcreasea purpurea* has erect or spreading, jointed, stiffish fleshy stems about a foot long. Its rather distantly spaced, toothless, oblong-lance-shaped, succulent leaves are 1½ to 6 inches or more in length and fringed with hairs. When grown in full sun they are rich violet-purple, in shade dull and much less attractive. The inch-wide, 3-petaled, orchid-pink flowers are in stalkless clusters cradled in pairs of boat-shaped leafy bracts at the shoot ends. Usually only one flower in each cluster is open at once. The others follow in succession.

How to grow. Easiest of plants to grow. Full sun needed for best color and blooms. From 50° F. to top summer heat OK, as is fair humidity to dry. Soil on the poor side rather than too fertile, with sharp drainage; let soil go nearly dry between waterings, then saturate. Cuttings root with extraordinary ease; take them from most colorful plants. Seeds usually give plants of inferior color.

30 ❧ The shrimp plant is commonly listed as *Beloperone guttata*. Only the most up-to-date gardeners know its botanical "in" name is now *Drejella guttata*. Its pink-bracted racemes of blooms are of a size, form, and color very suggestive of cooked shrimp—unless you have the variety called Yellow Queen or the Red King. The shrimp plant is native of Mex-

30. Shrimp Plant

ico. Wild and in tropical gardens, it becomes a shrub sometimes 8 feet or more tall. As a house plant it is ordinarily
not more than a foot or two high. Belonging to the acanthus
family, it is kin to the zebra plant and *Crossandra*. Thin-
stemmed and unless carefully pruned loose and straggly, the
shrimp plant has softly hairy leaves, egg-shaped in outline,
about an inch long. Its flower spikes, at the ends of the
branches, are 1½ to 3½ inches long, are composed of leaflike bracts (brick red in the typical kind) that overlap like
shingles. The white flowers peep from between these.

How to grow. Give it all the sun you can; keep night temperature above 50° F., humidity above 30%. Pot in any well-
drained, fertile soil; keep moist but let it dry on top before
watering. Repot in spring. Give well-rooted plants dilute
liquid fertilizer twice monthly spring through fall. Propagate
by cuttings (easy) late winter or spring. Except on those you
mean to let flower, pinch out tips off branches at 6 inches to
aid branching and shapeliness.

31. Spathiphyllum clevelandii

31   *Spathiphyllum clevelandii* is an easier-to-grow relative of the flamingo or tailflower, and so is kin with cala-
diums, calla-lilies, philodendrons, skunk cabbage, and all the
many other members of the arum family. A hybrid of species
from tropical South America, this kind is tolerant of difficult
environments. It will live for years, not necessarily flowering
abundantly, with less light than almost any other house plant.
It stands low humidities well although grows more lushly in

moister air. Even when out of bloom, it is attractive. An abundance of dark green foliage is typical. Its leaves have thinnish stalks and broadly lance-shaped blades with somewhat wavy margins, 9 to 12 inches long. As with most arums, the "flowers" are technically inflorescences. They consist of a rigid spikelike column with tiny flowers crowded along it and from its base a large, petal-like bract. In *Spathiphyllum clevelandii* the inflorescences are on long reedlike stems. The bracts don't surround the flower spike as do those of calla lilies and jack-in-the-pulpit, but stand free. They are pointed-lance-shaped, pure white with a green stripe down their backs, and 5 to 6 inches in length.

How to grow. Pot in rich soil with much organic matter; keep moist and give dilute liquid fertilizer every 14 days. Sponge grime off leaves now and then, or lay plant in bathtub. Repot in bigger pots spring or early summer. Ordinary house temperature, fair humidity, are OK. Give good light, some shade from summer sun, for flowering. Propagate by division.

32 🌺 Star-of-Bethlehem is the colloquial name in New England and some other parts of the United States for *Campanula isophylla*. Although considering the form of the flowers, this name is appropriate, it leads to confusion because entirely different plants of another genus, *Orinthogalum*, are well known by the same common name and likely have prior claim to it. Campanulas as a group are called bellflowers, but the blooms of this are not bell-like, so that is not obviously apt. Call it what you will, the sort under consideration is one of the loveliest of house plants. Unfortunately, it prospers only where summers, particularly nights, are fairly cool. Of trailing habit, this campanula is elegant in hanging baskets as well as pots. An evergreen perennial, native of Italy and belonging to the bellflower family, it has slender stems and alternate, more or less heart-shaped, toothed leaves up to 1½ inches across and downy or not. An inch or more wide, the starry blooms are lilac to clear blue, in one variety white.

How to grow. Easy to manage where summers are cool. Mix one part topsoil, one part organic matter, one part coarse sand or perlite, with a little bonemeal; keep well drained. Good sun, winter nights at 50° F., 60° F. by day, about 50% humidity; light shade from strongest sun in summer. Keep soil moderately moist. Fertilize occasionally summer, early fall. Cuttings root easily in sand, perlite, vermiculite, at 55 to 60° F. with shade from direct sun.

33 ❧ Sterptocarpuses (*Streptocarpus,* which sounds more like a disease) are elegant flowering plants, once known by the more beguiling, partly misleading name of Cape primroses. They aren't primroses, but the ancestors of modern hybrid kinds *are* natives of South Africa, once generalized as the Cape of Good Hope region. Streptocarpuses belong in the gesneria family, are kissing kin of African violets and gloxinias. There are many sorts. Probably the best are the "nymph" hybrids or which robust Constant Nymph was the first. Others include descriptively named White Nymph, Purple Nymph, Cobalt Nymph and so on. These are the easiest and most satisfactory streptocarpuses to grow. They have stemless clumps of evergreen, nearly strap-shaped, pebbly-surfaced, arching, spreading leaves each with a strong midvein. Most are about 6 inches long by 1 to 2 inches broad, bigger in "Constant Nymph." The plentiful wiry flower stalks sprout from the bases of the leaves, lift the blooms well above the foliage. Each carries up to 6 buds that open in succession. The flowers are nearly 3 inches long, narrowly trumpet-shaped, with 5 spreading petals forming an asymmetrical face. Those of Constant Nymph are clear blue.

How to grow. These do well in windows, indoor light gardens. Needs are like those of African violets' but less tolerant of aridity and heat. Nights of 55 to 65° F., days up to 80° F. are best. Little growth occurs if days go below 65° F., above 80° F. Good light, shade from summer sun, 50% humidity and up are needed. It helps to stand pots in tray of moist sand or gravel. Soil: well drained, generous organic matter, loosely packed to admit air to roots. Propagate by division, leaf cuttings, in spring.

34 ❧ The water hyacinth (*Eichhornia azurea*), the "million-dollar weed," is at least the "multimillion-dollar weed" for many millions have been spent in trying to control its takeover of canals and other waters in Florida and other warm lands. But this costly pest is beautiful in foliage and flower and can be grown indoors with greatest ease. Of the pickerel weed family, this is native of tropical and sub-tropical America. A floating evergreen aquatic, it has rosettes of leaves with fat, bulbous, pithy stalks and glossy, egg-shaped to nearly-circular blades 3 to 4 inches across. Erect and hyacinthlike, its flower spikes are of several to many 2-inch-wide, violet-colored blooms with, on the upper petal, a peacock-eye patch of bright blue with a yellow spot at its center. Individual flowers remain open for only a single day.

How to grow. As spawning cover in tropical fish tanks these seldom bloom, being out of intense light. Full sun, 55° F. and up, are needed. Plants can live unrooted, but last longer with a toehold. Put 2 to 3 inches clayey soil in gold-fish bowl or like container, cover with ½ inch coarse sand. Place saucer on sand, gently trickle in water not to disturb sand, remove saucer. Water depth: 4 to 6 inches. Float plants on surface; roots, handsome themselves, will find the soil.

35. Zebra Plant

35 ❧ The zebra plant, *Aphelandra squarrosa louisae,* a member of the acanthus family—is not new but it seems to have been "discovered" and promoted by commercial growers fairly recently. A spectacular ornamental, admired as much for foliage as flowers. The latter, carried in large, long-lasting terminal spikes, are yellow, with each bloom nestled in a bract almost as brightly colored. The slightly fleshy, broad-elliptic leaves taper to points, are 3 to 5 inches long. Rich green and glossy, they display herringbones of white veins. Alas, not an ideal house plant. Native of steamy forests in Brazil, the zebra plant adapts poorly to most American homes with their dry air, dehydrating drafts, and cold windows. As a gift or holiday plant, the zebra plant with care will remain in good condition for weeks or even months but only rarely will it survive, look well, and bloom on a more permanent basis. You may achieve the exception by growing it inside a terrarium where light is good, a 70° F. or higher temperature is constant, and atmospheric humidity is 70% or above.

How to grow. If you place it in an open room, keep away from drafts and radiators. Cover at night with a plastic bag, water freely with tepid water, fertilize sparingly monthly. Propagate by cuttings. Soil: well-drained, abundant organic matter.

Numbers 36–51 *are woody-stemmed plants, technically shrubs, that, if cared for properly, live for many years. Most can be grown to large sizes or, by pruning, can be kept very much smaller.*

36. Bush Allamanda

36 🌿 Bush allamanda (*Allamanda neriifolia*) is the only member of its genus suitable as a house plant. The others are all rampant vines, admired in the tropics for their wealth of gorgeous golden blooms but scarcely manageable indoors. The bush species is indeed a bush, not a vine. Outdoors in warm countries it may attain a height of 5 to 10 feet, but in pots 6 inches in diameter or bigger very respectable flowering examples 1½ to 3 feet high can be achieved. Native of Brazil, this has evergreen, oblongish leaves paler on their under than upper surfaces and 3 to 4 inches long. The flowers are charming miniatures of those borne by the grosser vining sorts. The blooms are a little more than an inch in length, golden yellow with greenish bases, and lightly striped on their insides with brownish-red. Botanically related to oleanders and vincas, the bush allamanda belongs to the dogbane family.

How to grow. About 50% humidity best; no less than 55° F. even on winter nights. Full sun best; part-day shade tolerable. Outdoors under a tree or a light porch ideal in summer. Pot in rich soil, repot or topdress every 12 to 24 months. Give dilute liquid fertilizer every 14 days spring through fall. For this period, water abundantly; less in winter, but never let it go dry. Prune to shape late winter or early spring, removing thin, crowded stems, shortening others. Cuttings root well in spring, early summer, in sand, vermiculite, perlite, in humid air at 70 to 75° F.

37. Angel's Trumpet

37 ❧ Angel's trumpet (*Datura suaveolens*), popular as an outdoor ornamental in warm countries, is native of Brazil. This evergreen shrub belongs with eggplants, potatoes, and tomatoes in the nightshade family, of the same genus as the Jimson weed, dangerously poisonous if its fruits or other parts are eaten. Growing 10 feet or more out of doors in warm climates in a large pot or tub, the angel's trumpet can be kept to 4 to 6 feet, but it has a fairly broad spread and needs room such as that of sunrooms and large windows. The leaves are pointed-egg-shaped, 6 to 12 inches long. Dan-

46

gling from the branches like great trumpets, the fragrant white blooms are 9 to 12 inches long.

How to grow. Propagate by cuttings in sand, perlite, etc., in humid, shaded air at 60 to 70° F. When rooted, put in small pots, sandy soil; later repot in bigger pots, less sandy soil; ultimately they may need pots 9 to 12 inches across. Soil: porous, equal parts good topsoil, organic matter, and coarse sand, grit or perlite, with bonemeal at 2 heaped teaspoonfuls to a pint. Late winter or spring, prune out weak twiggy shoots, shorten strong ones, repot if needed. Water freely spring through fall and give dilute liquid fertilizer every 14 days. Grow in sun or light shade at 55 to 60° F. nights, up to 75° F. days. You may set outdoors or on porch in light shade in summer. Stop fertilizing in fall; in winter water less, keep in cool, light place 45 to 55° F.

38 ❧ Azaleas—of the sorts sold by florists from Christmas to spring—are popular indoor decoratives and gift plants. Often they are so covered with beautiful pink, red, white, or parti-colored blooms that the plant bearing them is scarcely visible. Azaleas belong in the *Rhododendron* genus and are members of the heath family, needing acid, well-drained, always evenly moist soil. Florists' azaleas are evergreen shrubs, varieties and hybrids of species native to Eastern Asia. They have small to medium-sized elliptic leaves. The flowers range from small and funnel-shaped to much larger and saucer-shaped or, in double-flowered varieties, flattish and almost camellialike. When you have acquired an azalea in bloom, put it in a window away from radiators in a cool

38. Azalea

room where it will get good light but no direct sun other than in early morning or late afternoon. Water as often as needed to prevent the soil drying out.

How. to grow. Most of these sold each year die without blooming again; not easy house plants. To succeed with them do as follows. Pick off all faded blooms. At first sign of stout new growth repot into bigger well-drained pot. Mix one part good topsoil, one part leaf mold or peat moss, one part coarse sand or perlite, with dried cow manure one-tenth of entire mix. Pack firmly. Mist foliage 2 to 3 times daily. When there is no danger of nights below 50° F., set outdoors in light shade. In summer give dilute acid fertilizer every 14 days. Before frost bring into light window or sunroom with 40 to 50° F. nights, up to 60° F. days, humidity 50% up.

39 ❦ Blue plumbago (*Plumbago auriculata*, formerly *P. capensis*), popular outdoors in subtropical climates, is satisfactory indoors in sunrooms and large sunny windows where temperatures are not excessively high, especially at night from fall to spring. This is an evergreen, clambering shrub that, unless restrained, is likely to become too big for most indoor accommodations. A South African plant of the plumbago family, it has evergreen, more or less spoon-shaped leaves 1½ to 2 inches long. Its loose clusters of lovely azure-blue, phloxlike blooms are produced with great freedom in spring and summer. A variety with pure white flowers is also available.

39. Blue Plumbago

How to grow. Pot young plants in 6-inch pots; at 2 years or more they need 8 to 12 inch pots or tubs. Mix good topsoil, organic matter and coarse sand, grit, or perlite in equal parts, and add bonemeal, 2 heaped teaspoonfuls to the pint; pack firmly. Late winter, prune severely, especially side branches, and repot if needed. Water freely spring through fall, less in winter without letting go dry. Give well-rooted ones dilute liquid fertilizer twice monthly spring through fall. At start of winter, shorten stems moderately. In winter keep at 50 to 55° F. nights, up to 70° F. days, humidity of 30% and up. Propagate from cuttings in sand, perlite, etc., in humid air at 60 to 70° F.

40. Fleur d'Amour

40 ❧ Fleur d'amour, flower of love, is the colloquial name of *Ervatamia coronaria,* also sometimes known as *Tabernaemontana coronaria.* Presumably the delightful fragrance of its pure white gardenialike blooms gives reason for the popular name. It is also called crape-jasmine (not to be confused with Cape-jasmine, which is the gardenia), clavel de la India, East Indian rosebay, butterfly-gardenia, and Nero's crown. Native somewhere in the Old World tropics, this delightful evergreen shrub is much cultivated outdoors in warm, frostless climates, where it grows 6 feet and more. Although resembling a gardenia, it is not related to that plant but, since it belongs in the dogbane family, to allamandas and vincas. It is bushy, shrubby, and satisfactory indoors when 1 to 3 feet tall. It has elliptic to lance-shaped leaves 3 inches or so long, and, over a long period, a profusion of blooms 1½ to 2 inches in diameter. There are single- and double-flowered varieties and one with fringed petals.

How to grow. These do best in 50% humidity and higher; small ones thrive in large terrariums. Keep 55° F. minimum nights; full sun with light shade from hottest summer sun is best, as outdoors under a tree. Repot in spring in slightly acid soil: equal parts good topsoil, leaf mold or peat moss, sand or perlite, with a little bonemeal. Prune when repotting. Water freely spring through fall, more sparingly in winter. Give dilute liquid fertilizer twice monthly spring to fall; misting foliage 2 to 3 times daily is good. Cuttings root readily spring and early summer in sand, perlite, etc., in humid air, shaded from direct sun.

41 ❧ Fuchsias (*Fuchsia*), members of the evening primrose family, first came prominently to the attention of gardeners as the result of a sailor's gift to his mother. The sailor, name unknown, had brought from South America a small specimen of an unusual flowering plant. This was blooming in a window of his mother's home beside the Thames at Wapping when, in 1788, nurseryman James Lee of Hammer-

41. Fuchsia

smith passed, saw the plant and determined to buy it. The old lady at first refused to sell, but eventually 80 guineas in gold proved irresistible and she parted with her treasure with the promise that she was to be given the first 2 young plants propagated from it. Lee raised 300 new plants, all of which, except the 2 he gave the lady, he sold for a guinea each. Modern fuchsias are hybrids available in many varieties of shrubby evergreens. They have thinnish, egg-shaped, toothed leaves 1½ to 4 inches long and gracefully drooping blooms, sometimes fancifully called lady's eardrops, of various combinations of white, pinks, reds, purples, and violets. Each has 4 spreading colored sepals and 4—although double-flowered varieties more—petals. They are produced freely from spring to fall.

How to grow. Keep cool; 50° F. winter nights, up to 65° F. days, or stored semidormant in cool, dry cellar. In summer keep on shaded porch or under a tree. Root cuttings in sand, perlite, etc., in spring or summer in fairly humid air. Pinch out tips of shoots of young plants occasionally to induce branching. Pot in fertile, well-drained soil with some organic matter. Prune to shape and repot in spring, again in summer if needed. Spring to fall water freely, fertilize well-rooted ones twice monthly. Water sparingly in winter.

42 ❧ Gardenias. The name "gardenia" commemorates Alexander Garden, an 18th-century physician of Charleston, South Carolina. Gardenias, admired for their fragrant, pure white flowers, are sold in considerable numbers around Easter. Most of these sicken and die. Yet enough enthusiasts succeed in maintaining and flowering gardenias for years that the venturesome may try. Their prospects will be brighter if they pass up the usual large-bloomed florists' sorts identified as *G. veitchii* varieties and concentrate on the smaller-flowered, summer-blooming *G. jasminoides* or *G. florida,* popular as outdoor shrubs in the South. Gardenias, of the madder family, are evergreen shrubs of Old World tropics; those with which we are concerned of China.

How to grow. The winter-blooming greenhouse gardenia often comes from a very humid place to a much drier, draftier one with too-low night temperatures. Keep it out of drafts, well watered; mist foliage several times daily. Cover with a plastic bag at night. Keep away from windows in very cold weather. Treat as summer-blooming sorts (see below) except that in winter it needs a minimum of 65° F., high humidity, and a sunny place. Store summer-bloomers No-

42. Gardenia

vember to March in a light place at 40 to 55° F. Other times keep 60 to 70° F. nights, up to 85° F. days. Always provide 40% humidity or higher. Prune to shape, remove weak shoots, repot in fertile, porous, acid soil in spring. Spring to fall, water freely and give dilute acid liquid fertilizer weekly. Water sparingly; don't fertilize in winter. Propagate by summer cuttings in mix of sand or perlite with peat moss.

43 ❧ The glory bush or princess flower (*Tibouchina urvilleana*, often misidentified as *T. semidecandra*) is a stunning Brazilian that needs room and special conditions. Of the melastoma family, in the tropics it may grow 10 feet tall, but even when 2 feet high it blooms freely. Some growers discard plants after a year and raise new ones annually. The glory bush has lovely, often bronze, foliage. Its opposite, pointed-egg-shaped leaves 2 to 4 inches long are soft, velvety, hairy and have 3 or 5 prominent lengthwise veins. But its great joy is its stunning blooms. The pinkish buds open to flowers 3 to 4 inches or sometimes more across with 5 broad spreading petals of a glorious royal purple. At the centers of each are 10 curiously disposed spidery stamens. A succession of flowers is produced over from late summer well into the winter.

How to grow. Propagate from cuttings of firm, not hard, shoots planted in spring or summer in sand, perlite, or vermiculite at 70° F. Keep shaded in highly humid air. Pot rooted cuttings in small pots in sandy, peaty soil. Soon after, pinch out tips just above third pair of leaves. Repeat this with branches after they have 2 to 3 pairs of leaves. Repot in rich, porous soil in large containers as growth requires. Keep in bright light, shaded from strongest summer sun; 50 to 55° F. winter nights up to 70° F. days, warmer in summer; humidity 50%; soil always moderately moist. Spring to fall, give well-rooted ones dilute liquid fertilizer every 14 days. Prune and repot or topdress late winter or spring.

43. Glory Bush

44 ❧ Chinese hibiscus, rose-of-China, or shoeblack flower (*Hibiscus rosa-sinensis*) is plentiful in gardens in Hawaii and most other warm countries. There are at least 1,000 varieties, in a wide range of flower colors. Some have double blooms and one sort, *H. r. cooperi*, has leaves variegated with green, crimson, pink, and white. The red flowers of this last are smaller and less brilliant than those of kinds with plain green leaves. Derivatives of a tropical Asian, probably Chinese species, these hibiscuses are, because of their size, suitable only for sunrooms and large windows. They are usually 3 to 4 feet or more tall and bushy before they bloom. Belonging to the mallow family, they are relatives of hollyhocks, cotton, and the hardy rose-of-sharon. They have woody stems, narrowly to broadly egg-shaped, toothed leaves 3 to 4½ inches long. Their strikingly showy flowers, in brilliant reds, pinks, yellows, orange shades, and whites, are 4 to 9 inches across, have 5 flaring petals or in double varieties more. From the center of the singles is thrust a long column of stamens. The blooms last one day only, open in succession over a long period. Soon after falling they become mushy and can be used for polishing shoes, hence "shoeblack flower."

How to grow. These need winter nights at 55° F. or higher, up to 70° F. days, 40% humidity. Prune established plants late winter or spring, thinning out weak shoots, shortening others to limit plant's size. At this time, repot if needed, or prick away some surface soil and replace with a rich mix. Water freely spring to fall, moderately in winter. Fertilize well-rooted ones spring to fall. Cuttings of firm, not hard, shoots root easily in sand, perlite, etc., in humid, shady environment.

45 ❧ Hydrangeas (*Hydrangea macrophylla*), popular spring-flowering florists' gift and decorative plants, are tricky to manage as permanent house plants although if facilities are available for caring for them properly through the summer and during their winter dormancy this can be done. Most people accept them as handsome transients to enjoy while in flower; perhaps to be planted outdoors to develop into sizeable summer-blooming shrubs. They thrive well near the ocean. These plants are varieties of species native to Japan. Belonging to the saxifrage family, they have opposite, broadly egg-shaped, large-toothed leaves and big showy heads of white, pink, blue, or lavender-blue flowers. White-flowered sorts always have white blooms. The color of others varies with the character of the soil and water, pink if alkaline, blue if acid, intermediate if near neutral.

How to grow. To keep blooming gift plants best, put in window or cool room; keep soil constantly moist. To plant outdoors later, continue this treatment until frost is past; plant in sun or part shade in fertile, fairly moist soil. It you want to flower a plant indoors the next year, prune out old flowering shoots after it has bloomed; retain a few strong news ones; take plant from pot, prick away much old soil, repot in larger pot in porous, fertile soil. When frost is past, sink pot to rim outdoors in sand, earth, or the like, and keep well watered. After first light fall frost, bring indoors, store at 30 to 50° F. with little or no water until February. Then put plant in light window in coolish room. Resume watering;

after foliage develops, give dilute liquid fertilizer each 7 to 10 days. Propagation easy by summer cuttings.

46 ❧ India and Yeddo Hawthorns are *Rhaphiolepis indica* and *R. umbellata* respectively. A hybrid between them is *R. delacouri*. In addition, there are excellent named varieties of India hawthorn. In California and other mild, dryish climates these are popular outdoor shrubs. In small sizes, they are very worthwhile for sunrooms and sunny windows where temperatures are not excessive. Like true hawthorns (*Crataegus*), they belong in the rose family. India hawthorn belies its popular and botanical names, since it is native to China, not India. Yeddo hawthorn is Japanese. Both are evergreen shrubs, the first up to 5 feet tall, the other sometimes twice as high. In containers they can be maintained for many years at 2 to 3 feet. Their leaves are alternate, elliptic, toothed or toothless, 1½ to 3 inches or somewhat more long. The flowers, those of the India hawthorn especially, resembling small apple blossoms, are in considerable clusters. Those of India hawthorn are about ½ inch across and pale to deep pink. The Yeddo hawthorn has larger, pure white, fragrant blooms. Hybrids are intermediate. The small, hard, black, berrylike fruits last for a long time.

How to grow. Conditions suiting orange and other citrus trees are good. Sunny location, 30% humidity, well-drained containers, fertile, loamy soil: one part good topsoil, one part organic matter, one part coarse sand, grit or perlite. Add 2 heaped teaspoonfuls bonemeal to each pint of mix, 1/10 part by bulk of dried cow manure. As long as soil is porous and nourishing feel free to vary this formula. Prune to shape, repot in spring if needed. Keep at 40 to 50° F. winter nights, up to 65° F. days. Water spring to fall, moderately in winter. Fertilize occasionally in summer. Propagate by cuttings of fairly firm shoots in summer.

47 ❧ Ixoras (*Ixora*) are flowering shrubs very familiar to southern Florida, Hawaii, and such warm climates. They make good house plants in much smaller sizes than they assume in the tropics, but they still need pots 6 inches across or bigger, and they need largeish windows. To bloom freely, they need full sun with just a suspicion of shade during the brightest summer months. Ordinary house temperatures never below 60° F. are suitable. Humidity of 50% or more is desirable, but for periods they will get along with less. Ixoras belong in the madder family. Natives of the Old World trop-

.ics, ixoras have rather leathery, more or less elliptic leaves, usually 3 to 6 inches long but sometimes bigger. They are opposite or in circles of 3 or 4. The small flowers, red, orange-red, yellow, or white are in rather crowded, up-facing clusters of many. Each bloom has a long slender tube and 4 or 5 spreading petals.

How to grow. These need acid soil; in alkaline soil, leaves go yellow with only veins green. Remedy this with chelated iron from a garden supplier, following directions with package. Propagate from firm, not hard, shoots in sand, perlite, etc., at 70 to 75° F., slightly humid air. When cutting roots are 1 to 1½ inches, put in small pots in sandy, peaty soil. Keep newly potted plants shaded and humid. When they have recovered from transplanting shock, nip out tips to aid branching; repeat with branches that develop. With established plants, keep soil moderately moist, give dilute liquid fertilizer every 7 to 10 days spring to fall. Mist or spray foliage daily.

48 🌿 Lantanas (*Lantana*) are pestiferous weeds in Hawaii and some other tropical countries, but those are sorts inferior to the beautiful horticultural varieties. The garden sorts are complex hybrids of more gangling species native to the warm Americas. Botanically, lantanas belong to the verbena family. Evergreen, sometimes prickly shrubs, they bloom when very small, more or less continuously afterward. By pruning, pot specimens are generally held to heights of 9 to 12 inches but can be had considerably taller. The trailing or weeping lantana is good for hanging baskets. Lantanas have opposite, toothed, hairy, usually wrinkled, pointed, egg-shaped leaves 1 to 3 inches long. When rubbed, they emit a disagreeable odor. The little flowers—white, cream, deep yellow, orange, bronze, pink, red, or lavender-purple—are crowded in stalked verbenalike heads 1 to 2 inches across.

How to grow. Raising from seed produces inferior plants. Instead, root cuttings late winter to early summer in sand, perlite, etc., in humid shade at 70° F. and up. Pot rooted cuttings singly in small pots. At 3 to 4 inches tall pinch out tips; repeat this now and then to keep plant bushy. Repot as growth requires. Use porous, not over-rich soil, packed firmly. Grow in full sun at 60° F. and up. Average house humidity OK. Keep soil evenly moist; fertilize occasionally, but don't overdo—or you'll get rank growth instead of blooms. In fall, prune partway back, store in light cellar in

27. Pentas lanceolata (a Variety)

28. Poinsettia

32. Star-of-Bethlehem

33. Cape Primrose

34. Water Hyacinth (growing in Florida)

44. Chinese Hibiscus

45 and 59. Hydrangea and Easter Lily

46. India and Yeddo Hawthorns

47. Ixora (Super King Variety)

48. Lantana

49. Natal Plum (in Fruit)

53. Amaryllis

56. Cyclamen

58. Devil's Tongue

60. Flowering Onion

62. Gloxinia

62. Gloxinia (Double-flowered)

63. Hyacinth

66. Reichsteineria leucophylla

66. Reichsteineria cardinalis

68. Tulip

71. Crassula (Morgan's Beauty Variety)

72. Crown of Thorns

76. Moon Cactus

dryish condition at about 50° F. In spring, shake free of old soil, prune further, repot.

49 ❧ The Natal plum (*Carissa grandiflora*) is not a plum but an attractive, easily grown member of the dogbane family; a relative of allamandas, oleanders, and vincas. Native to South Africa, this evergreen shrub has usually strong, 2-pronged spines. Its glossy, broadly elliptic to egg-shaped, leathery leaves are 1 to 3 inches long. The fragrant, starry flowers, about 2 inches across, have 5 spreading, white, slightly twisted petals that give a pinwheel appearance to the blooms. They are mostly in clusters near the branch ends and are succeeded by plum-shaped red fruits 1 to 2 inches long that remain attractive for a long time. In the tropics these are used for a sauce like cranberry sauce. In warm countries the typical form of the natal plum may grow to 18 feet and, when trimmed, forms formidable hedges. For house plant dwarf varieties, the two best known are "Boxwood Beauty" and *Carissa grandiflora nana compacta* which is without spines. These are lower with spreading stems, small foliage and blooms; leaves are closer together.

How to grow. Needs little skill. Any fairly fertile, well-drained soil kept evenly moist, not wet. Keep in sunny window or one with a little part-day shade. Ordinary house temperatures suit; down to 50° F. nights OK. Humidity 30% and up; misting foliage on bright days good for growth. Fertilize well-rooted ones spring to fall. Prune to shape; repot late winter or early spring. More pruning of exuberant shoots may be needed in summer. Propagate from cuttings in sand, perlite, etc., in humid air 60 to 70° F. To keep dwarfed, don't raise from seeds.

50 ❧ The pineapple-guava (*Feijoa sellowina*) is admirable for a sunroom or sunny window in a cool room. In warm countries the fruits of this South American species of the myrtle family are esteemed for eating, but they are rarely developed on plants grown indoors. An evergreen shrub up to 15 feet or more tall in the open in favored climates, this can be kept to 2 to 3 feet or even lower in containers. It has opposite, oblongish to elliptic leaves 2 to 3 inches long, green above, on their undersides clothed with a felt of silvery-grayish hairs. The long-stalked flowers are solitary, 1 to 1½ inches across. They have four spreading petals, white-hairy on their outsides, their insides plum-purple. There is a central bunch of long stamens.

How to grow. Coolish winter temperatures make for easy growing: 45 to 50° F. nights to 60° F. days, humidity 30% up. Soil: fairly fertile, well drained. Old plants in largeish containers need repotting every few years only; young ones not full grown every two years. Prune to shape yearly in spring; also repot then. Pack soil firmly. Full sun is best for good shoots and bloom. Water freely spring to fall, less in winter; give dilute liquid fertilizer twice monthly spring to fall. Raise from seed in sandy soil at about 50° F., or from cuttings in sand, perlite, etc., same temperature.

50. Pineapple-Guava

51 ❧ The sweet olive (*Osmanthus fragrans*) is not an olive but a related plant esteemed for its deliciously perfumed tiny blooms, borne throughout the year but chiefly in late winter and spring. The fragrance is much like that of orange blossom. A single plant will scent a whole room. The flower buds are used to scent China tea. Native from Japan to the Himalayas, this is an evergreen shrub or tree that grows in mild climates to 25 feet or more. As an indoor plant it can be held to 2 to 3 feet, or higher if desired. The leaves are elliptic to oblong-lance-shaped, toothed or not, 3 to 4 inches long. The white to yellowish blooms, in loose clusters from the leaf axils, are short-tubular and have 4 spreading petals. The sweet olive *does* belong to the olive family.

51. Sweet Olive

How to grow. Easy to manage if given enough light, kept coolish, and well pruned (tends to be scraggly, sparsely foliaged). Any fertile, well-drained soil, moderately moist. Except for young plants, repotting is every few years; repot young yearly or as needed. Pot in spring after main flowering is over; at same time prune, whether repotting or not. Thin out weak, crowded shoots to shape and include branching. Keep in good light, shaded from strong summer, 30% humidity and up. Keep at 45 to 55° F. winter nights, up to 65° F. days. Propagate in summer by cuttings of firm shoots in sand, perlite, etc. Plants may be put outdoors in summer.

Numbers 52–69 *are plants with bulbs or tubers. Some can be grown permanently indoors, others for one season only. All have a period of dormancy (resting period) when they are without foliage.*

---

52 ❧ Achimenes (*Achimenes*), pronounced ak-**im**-en-eez, is the singular and plural of the name of a group of African violet relatives of singular beauty. They belong in the gesnerid family. Native from Mexico to tropical America, there are about 50 species. Here we are chiefly concerned with splendid hybrids developed from them. These have curi-

52. Achimenes

ous worm- or caterpillar-like rhizomes approximately an inch long, and slender, erect, hairy stems with equally hirsute, short-stalked, toothed, egg-shaped leaves 2 to 4 inches or so long, in pairs, three, or fours. The slender-tubed flowers have oblique faces, suggestive of pansies, up to nearly 2 inches across. They range from pure white through lavenders and pinks to richest purples and violets and, more especially among the species, some with yellow, orange, and red blooms. Achimenes don't prosper in polluted atmospheres, but elsewhere they are adaptable as window plants and for indoor light gardens. They bloom in summer.

How to grow. Rhizomes are stored though winter in pots in which plants grow. In spring shake rhyzomes free of soil, separate, and plant an inch apart, ½-inch deep, in 3-inch layer of peat moss or vermiculite. Water; put where temperature is about 70° F. When shoots are 2 inches tall, put 4 to a pot 5 inches across, 6 to each 6-inch pot. Use nourishing, porous soil with ⅓ organic matter, packed softly, yielding to finger pressure. Grow in light window at 60 to 65° F. nights, up to 75° F. days. Humidity 50% or higher. Give light shade from intense summer sun. Keep soil moderately moist. Give dilute liquid fertilizer weekly till late summer. In fall, gradually lengthen times between soakings, then stop watering; store over winter at 50-55° F. Propagate by seed, by separating rhyzomes, or from cuttings.

53 ❧ Amaryllis (*Hippeastrum*). The approved botanical name of these plants is *Hippeastrum*. Amaryllis may be employed as a common name but the botanical genus *Amaryllis* is a quite different South African plant, though both are of the amaryllis family. As wildlings, hippeastrums inhabit only tropical America. Bulbs of hybrids are sold by garden centers and similar outlets, and mail-order houses. In bloom probably the most spectacular of house plants, hippeastrums have large bulbs, and long, strap-shaped, fleshy leaves. They send up in winter or early spring stout, hollow stalks, mostly with two to four magnificent lilylike, trumpet-shaped blooms often 7 to 8 inches in diameter; colors are dark red, brilliant red, orange-red, pink, white-striped, or feathered with pink or red, or pure white. The foliage develops before, with, or after the flowers.

How to grow. Buy a good bulb in fall or early winter; follow procedures and you can hardly fail. With bulb you'll get an incipient stalk and blooms. Plant bulb in a well-drained pot 2 inches wider than diameter of bulb. Position bulb with upper half above surface. Pack soil firmly, water thoroughly, and put in a dark place at 50 to 55° F. When a fat bud emerges, remove pot to sunny place, shaded the first few days, at 65 to 72° F. Keep soil moist. The blooms develop rapidly. After flowering ends, continue watering and, with old but not first-year bulbs, fertilize twice monthly to fall. Then dry by lengthening times between soakings; stop watering at last and store over winter at 50 to 55° F. At start of new growth, season repot or topdress old plants. Propagate by offset bulbs or seeds.

54 ❧ Tuberous begonias (*Begonia tuberhybrida*) of the begonia family bear in summer gorgeous, large to immense single or double blooms, those of some varieties fancifully frilled or crested. They come in a wide array of pinks, reds, creams and yellows as well as bicolors and whites, 3 to 8 inches across. They are hybrids of species native to the high South American Andes; this accounts for their preference for coolness. Where nights are cool, even though days are hot, they can be superb. Tuberous begonias have tubers, underground, bulblike organs from which in spring grow roots and succulent, leafy, flower-bearing stems. In fall, tops and roots die and the tubers become dormant. The leaves are large, asymmetrically heart-shaped, and toothed.

How to grow. You can raise from seed; it's simpler to

54. Tuberous Begonia

begin with bought tubers. Obtain these 1 to 1½ inches in diameter. Plant in spring in leaf mold or peat moss mixed with sand or perlite; place hollow side up, tops exposed. Keep moist, not wet, at about 70° F. in some shade. At 2 to 3 inches pot in well-drained loose, porous, fertile soil with much organic matter. Tops of tubers go ½ inch below surface. Use 4-inch pots; repot in larger when these are root-filled. Give good light out of strong sun, 60 to 65° F. nights, 75° F. days. You may put on porch or in outdoor shade in summer. Keep soil evenly moist; give well-rooted ones dilute liquid fertilizer to fall. Stake and tie for support. Pinch out 2 side buds of each group of 3 to get biggest blooms. In fall, gradually reduce watering. When foliage dies, store tubers over winter at 50° F.

55 ❧ The Bermuda buttercup (*Oxalis pes-caprea*) is often listed under its now-obsolete name of *O. cernua*. Naturalized in Bermuda, Florida, the south of France, and other warm regions, it is actually a native of South Africa. Easy to grow, it produces a profusion of clear yellow blooms for several weeks in spring. It has scaly bulbs and very long-stalked, shamrocklike leaves each with three reverse-heart-shaped, often-spotted leaflets about an inch wide and nearly as long. The fragrant, nodding blooms, 1 to 1½ inches wide, are in loose heads at the ends of very long, leaflets stalks. In the single variety they have 5 petals. Those of the double-flowered sort have more. These plants belong in the oxalis family.

55. Bermuda Buttercup

How to grow. Start in fall with a few bulbs from a dealer of friend; plant bulbs 2 inches apart, 1 inch deep, in 5- to 6-inch pots. Use mix of topsoil, sand or perlite, organic matter, and bonemeal at 2 teaspoonfuls to a pint. Water soil thoroughly; put pot in window at 50 to 55° F. nights, to 65° F. days. Give shade at first; when shoots appear give full sun. Water to keep soil just moist at first, more when foliage and roots develop. Give dilute liquid fertilizer every 7 to 10 days from February on. When flowering is over, increase time between waterings until foliage is dead; stop watering. Store over summer in cool, dry, airy place. Repot in fall.

56 ✿ Cyclamens are mostly purchased as temporary decorations and gifts. After flowering it is usual to discard them, but some enthusiasts succeed in blooming them in successive years. It is not easy. The miniature species *Cyclamen neapolitanum* is easier to keep permanently than the bigger sorts. Modern varieties are developments of *Cyclamen persicum* a native from Greece to Syria. They belong to the primrose family. Cyclamens have bulblike organs (corms) but these are not naturally replaced each year by new ones but growing bigger annually. From the tops of the corms sprout a forest of long-stalked, roundish, often prettily marbled leaves and a large number of white, pink, or red blooms produced over a period of many weeks. Each flower has its own stalk that carries it well above the foliage. The blooms are beautifully and unusually shaped.

Their 5 petals stream backward, as one author says, like the "ears of a hare in flight" or those of an angry horse.

How to grow. You will probably acquire a plant in bloom; keep it in a window with diffuse light at 45 to 55° F. nights to 65° F. days; 50% humidity at least. Pick faded blooms promptly. All this prolongs health and blooming. When flowering finishes and leaves begin to die naturally, gradually lengthen periods between waterings, finally cease. Store until early September in warm, dry, airy place. Then free plant from pot, prick away as much old earth as possible, replace with new, fertile earth. Resume watering. Grow in north-facing window in a cool room at 50% humidity or more. Mist foliage daily. When roots fill pot, give weekly dilute liquid fertilizer.

57. Narcissus

57 ❧ Daffodils and other narcissuses are easy to bloom indoors long before outdoor displays appear. By planting several pots of selected sorts and bringing them into forcing temperatures in succession, you can have flowers from Thanksgiving to Easter or later. These plants belong in the genus *Narcissus,* a member of the amaryllis family occurring natively in Europe and temperate Asia. These have bulbs, narrowly strap-shaped, deciduous leaves, and solitary or clustered flowers atop leafless hollow stalks. The prevailing flower colors are many shades of yellow and white, but some varieties have pinkish to apricot-colored blooms and in some the crown is stained or rimmed with red. The latter is the center cuplike or trumpet-shaped feature of the flower. Sorts with large trumpets are called daffodils—or in some parts of the United States, less correctly, jonquils. Short-crowned kinds are known as narcissuses, a name that may also be used for daffodils. Culturally these plants fall into two groups, hardy and nonhardy. The first includes trumpet daffodils, poets' narcissus, and most other sorts. These survive cold winters and bloom outdoors in spring. Nonhardy varieties are "Paper White," "Grand Soleil d'Or," and "Chinese sacred lilies," which in mild, frost-free climates flower outdoors in winter.

How to grow. To force hardy narcissuses, proceed as with hyacinths, but omit the period of darkness after first bringing them indoors. Also, if possible, grow them until their flowers open in temperatures no higher than about 60° F. Forced bulbs planted later in the garden will in future years give good outdoor displays. Bulbs of nonhardy kinds may be planted closely together in pots of soil or in bowls filled with pebbles or gravel and water, with the upper two-thirds of the bulbs standing above the water. From the time of planting keep them in a sunroom or sunny window where the temperature is 45 to 50° F. nights, 60° F. days. When the flowers begin to open, the plants may be transferred for display to warmer quarters.

58 🌿 The devil's tongue or snake palm (*Amorphophallus rivieri*) is a curiosity. But for one drawback, it would doubtless be grown oftener for its magnificent foliage and strange blooms. For a couple of days at the height of flowering it emits a powerful, disgusting, stench. In the wild this attracts carrion flies to pollinate the flowers. The only "out" during the plant's brief period of offense is to banish it to some out-of-the-way place. Native to Vietnam, this member of the arum family has a large, bulblike tuber. From later summer or fall until January, or later this is dormant. At the end of its dormancy if of blooming size it sends up an inflorescence that resembles a huge calla lily. It tops a stalk 2 to 4 feet tall, and consists of a central spike (spadix) on which the true flowers, not showy and of insignificant size are borne, the females toward its base, the males above, and a foot-long bract (spathe) that forms a trumpet around the spadix. Spadix and spathe are sinister vinous-purple. Succeeding or instead of an inflorescence a single leaf develops. This has a handsomely mottled thick erect stalk 3 to 4 feet tall, topped by a huge umbrellalike blade dissected into numerous leaflets.

How to grow. Plant tuber in a large pot or tub in fertile soil containing generous organic matter. Keep dry at 50° to 60° F. when dormant, moist at 60° F. or above when in flower or leaf. Give dilute liquid fertilizer weekly from when the leaf begins to spread its "umbrella" until it starts to die naturally. Propagation is by offsets.

59   Easter lilies (varieties of *Lilium longiflorum*) are popular but plants that, having bloomed indoors, will not do so again. In regions not appreciably colder than New York City they can after flowering be planted outside to bloom again in summer and in succeeding years. The Easter lily is not old in cultivation. Until its advent, the white madonna lily *(L. candidum)* of Europe was the lily of Christian religious significance. That is the one depicted in early paintings of the Virgin. The Easter lily grows on Okinawa and other islands to the south of Japan, in pockets of humus in coral rock. Bulbs first were collected and sent to England in 1819. From there they were taken to Bermuda where a great bulb-growing industry developed. This ended when a virus disease ravaged the bulb fields. Later Japan and eventually Oregon, Georgia, Florida, and Louisiana became the chief commercial sources of bulbs. Easter lilies have bulbs built of scales which overlap like shingles, erect, leafy stems, and few to several intensely fragrant, white, trumpet-shaped bulbs. They belong in the lily family.

How to grow. Although a few enthusiasts report raising specimens from bulbs to bloom, this is not generally practicable. Upon receipt of a blooming plant soak its soil with water and locate it in bright light but not direct sun. It will last longer at 60° and 70° F., not higher. Let soil dry but not completely between soakings. When blooming is past water regularly, give dilute liquid fertilizer every 7 to 10 days. When nights are a stable 50° F., plant outdoors in deep, fertile soil, with top of bulb 5 to 6 inches below surface.

60   Flowering onions (*Allium*) belong in the same genus as edible onions, leeks, and chives, all members of the lily family. Two natives of the Mediterranean region, *A. triquetrum* and *A. neapolitanum* are good ornamental pot plants for cool windows and sunrooms. These have small bulbs and 2 to 5 narrowly strap-shaped leaves 4 to 8 inches long. Those of *A. triquetrum* go to 1¼ inches wide, those of *A. nea-*

politanum, no more than ¾ inch. The leafless flower stalks, 3-angled, and 6 to 12 inches long, terminate in a head of ½-inch-wide, starry, 6-petaled, white blooms, those of *A. triquetrum* erect or nodding, those of the other facing upward. All parts of the plants if bruised emit an odor of onions, but that of *A. neapolitanum* is less powerful.

How to grow. In early fall plant several bulbs in 5-inch pot, with space between them equal to their diameters. Have tips just below surface. Firm soil. This should be equal parts topsoil, organic matter, and sand, grit, or perlite, with 2 heaped teaspoonfuls bonemeal to each pint. Water potted bulbs often enough to keep soil from drying, but with restraint until roots and foliage are well developed; then be more generous. Keep at about 50° F. winter nights, to 60° F. days. In February begin giving dilute liquid fertilizer every 7 to 10 days. After flowering, when leaves start to die naturally, gradually dry by increasing times between waterings. Finally stop watering and store in cool place until fall. Then repot and start again.

61 ✿ Freesias (*Freesia*), among the most deliciously fragrant of house plants, are, alas, not for everyone. Unless you can give them a very cool, sunny location during their fall-to-spring growing season, forego them. But if you have

a sunroom or a south-facing window, not above 50° F. nor below 40° F. at night, you can grow these beautiful flowers. Modern varieties come in a wide spectrum of flower colors as well as pure white. They are developments of species native to South Africa. Of the iris family, they have bulblike organs called corms. These, dormant through the summer, start into growth in fall. Then they develop erect stems with a few narrow leaves 1 to 1½ feet long, and wiry, branched flower stems about the same length. The funnel-shaped blooms face upward. The portion of the stalk that carries them is held horizontally.

How to grow. You can raise these from seed sown in sandy soil in early fall, but these take 2 to 3 years to bloom; better to buy bulbs. Get them at least ⅝ inches in diameter. Plant them in September or October, 2 inches apart in 5- to 6-inch pots of sandy, fertile soil. Cover one inch deep; water. Keep watering moderately until pots are root-filled, then freely. When flower spikes begin to show, give weekly dilute liquid fertilizer. After flowering, remove faded blooms; keep watering until foliage begins to die, then taper off and finally cease. Store over summer in cool, dry, airy place, in soil in which they grew, or take them from it. (If the latter they can be hung from ceiling in old stockings.) Replant in fall, before any signs of new growth. In planting, keep bulbs and offsets of same sizes together.

62 ❧ Gloxinias, as the name is used by gardeners, are varieties of *Sinningia speciosa*. The *Gloxinia* of botanists is related but quite different. Modern horticultural gloxinias are the most resplendent members of the gesneria family. In magnificence of bloom they far excel their relative the African violet, but are neither as adaptable nor as easy to grow, though by no means impossible. The species from which modern sorts have been bred is an inhabitant of Brazil. Gloxinias have bulblike tubers from which annual roots and foliage develop. They may or may not have short stems. The spreading leaves are oblong-elliptic to oblong-heart-shaped, softly hairy, 6 to 10 inches long. The velvety flowers are truly gorgeous. Trumpet-shaped to cup-shaped, they have 5 flaring lobes (petals). Their colors include pinks, reds, lavenders, blues, purples, and white. Some are bi-colored. There are single- and double-flowered varieties.

How to grow. You can raise from seed sown scarcely covered in late winter or spring in sandy, peaty soil or on milled sphagnum, at 70 to 75° F. in humid air. You can also propagate by cuttings from portions of leaves and by cutting tubers into pieces. Home growers usually begin with bought tubers. These should be 1½ inches in diameter, firm and plump. Plant smooth, round side downward, upper side level with surface. Use loose, coarse, fertile soil with generous organic matter. Pack moderately. Grow in light shaded from strong sun, minimum night temperature 60° F., humidity 50% up. Keep soil evenly moist. Give dilute liquid fertilizer weekly when roots fill pots. After blooming, when leaves begin to die gradually reduce water, then dry completely. Store through dormant season at 55 to 60° F.

63 ❧ Hyacinths, most fragrant of spring-flowering bulbs, are among the easiest to force into early bloom. From early February until flowers come outdoors you can have a succession of magnificent spikes of white, pink, red, lavender, blue, purple, and soft yellow flowers. Modern hyacinths are varieties of *Hyacinthus orientalis* of the liy family, a native from Greece to Syria and Asia Minor. Varieties have been cultivated for centuries by flower lovers, among them Napoleon's Empress Josephine, who cherished these fragrant hyacinths in her garden at Malmaison.

How to force. As early in fall as they are available, buy from a reliable dealer plump, heavy bedding size or bigger bulbs. Avoid small ones and don't wait until bulbs have been in the store for weeks. Pot immediately in ordinary soil, tips just above soil, one bulb to a 4- to 5-inch pot, 3 or more in larger. Water thoroughly, bury pots outdoors under 8-inch layer of sand, peat moss, or sawdust. When this freezes to an inch or two, cover with thick layer of leaves, straw or evergreen branches. In mid-January or later, at 2-week intervals, bring one or more pots inside. Keep in absolute darkness until spikes push well up, then gradually accustom them to a sunny window. Growth is sturdier at under 70° F. Water liberally. Forced bulbs won't force again but may grow well outdoors the following year if planted outside.

64 ❧ The Jacobean, St. James, or Aztec lily (*Sprekelia formosissima*) is not a lily but a member of the amaryllis family. From them it differs in never bearing more than one bloom on a stalk, in the 6 petals of the handsome flowers being of markedly different widths and 2 of them curling in almost sinister fashion. Native of Mexico and Guatemala, this fine ornamental was cultivated in Europe as early as

64. Jacobean Lily

1593. Its blooms brought to mind the red crosses embroidered on the cloaks of the Knights of St. James of Calatrova. It has a large, black, egg-shaped bulb. Its narrowly strap-shaped leaves up to a foot long are produced with or a little before or after the flowers. The gorgeous red blooms, 4 inches across, top hollow stalks a foot or more long.

How to grow. The bulbs are dormant September to February: store in their pots in dry place at 50 to 60° F.; a cellar, dark or light, is OK. As soon as a bud starts pushing through, replace some surface soil with new or repot. Put plants in sun at normal house temperature, not less than 40% humidity. Start normal watering. When repotting (every 3 to 4 years) use fertile, well-drained soil with moderate organic matter. Pack firmly, ⅓ of bulb above surface. After flowering: water repotted plants generously; plants not repotted get weekly fertilizing until leaf growth is finished. In September start increasing times between waterings; finally stop entirely. Store for winter. New plants can be had by repotting offset bulbs.

65 Pineapple flowers (*Eucomis*) are so called because the topknots of short leaves that crown their flower spikes look very like those on pineapples. Eucomises are not as well known as they should be. Easy to grow, they belong to the lily family, are natives of South Africa. There are several species. The one pictured here is *E. comosa,* sometimes called *E. punctata.* Unlike the majority of South African bulbs pineapple flowers make their growth from spring through fall and bloom in summer. They are dormant in winter. Bulbs are 2 to 3 inches in diameter. Out of their tops sprout a circle of several wavy strap-shaped leaves a foot or more long by 2 to 3 inches wide. From the center of these a stout, erect flowering stalk, its upper half a thick, cylindrical spike of pale green or greenish-white starry blooms, rises to a height of 2 feet or so.

How to grow. Pot bulbs in spring, tops just peering out of surface, in loamy, fertile, free-draining soil—one part topsoil, one part coarse sand or perlite, one part organic matter, with 2 teaspoonfuls of bonemeal to a pint of mix. Pack firmly. Repot in spring every 3 to 5 years; intervening springs prick away surface soil and replace with fresh. Put plants in sun, keep soil evenly moist. Cool house temperatures, 30% humidity and up are OK. Fertilize well-rooted ones mildly spring to late summer. In fall reduce watering gradually, stop when foliage dies. Store dry in 40 to 50° F. Propagate by offsets, by seeds, by using leafy crowns as cuttings.

65. Pineapple Flowers

66 ❧ Rechsteinerias were long known (and still some-times are) by the name gesnerias, but research clearly indi-cates that gesnerias belongs to a different but related group of plants. Both *Rechsteineria* and *Gesneria* are members of the gesneria family, as are African violets, flame violets, gloxinias, and the lipstick plant. It is easy to distinguish rechsteinerias from gesnerias. The first have tubers, and leaves in opposite pairs or circles of 3 or 4; gesnerias are without tubers, have alternate leaves. Rechsteinerias are not well suited for open rooms but do well in terrariums and indoor light gardens. With clear green foliage and bright red blooms decidedly "Christmasy" in aspect, *R. cardinalis* is native to Brazil. This has stems from 4 to 10 inches tall and pairs of softly hairy, heart-shaped leaves with round-toothed edges. The hairy, tubular, brilliant cardinal red blooms are numerous, 1½ to 2 inches long, and displayed well above the foliage. Quite different *R. leucotricha*, some-times known as Brazilian edelweiss, is about as big, has densely silvery-white-hairy leaves usually in circles of 4 and clusters of salmon-pink to salmon-red, tubular blooms about 1¼ inches in length.

How to grow. Sow seeds without soil covering on sandy peaty soil or milled sphagnum kept moist, or propagate from cuttings. Pot seedlings or rooted cuttings rather loosely in soil with plenty of organic matter plus grit or perlite; add a little crushed charcoal. Shade from strong sun; keep humidity 50% and up, temperature at 65° F. and up. Repot old tubers and start them into growth in spring. Winters, store in soil they grew in at 50 to 55° F.

67 ❧ The Scarborough lily (*Vallota speciosa*) is an inter-esting amaryllis relative, the only member of its genus. Native to South Africa, this is a late-summer to early-winter bloomer. It is distinguishable from more common amaryllises (hippeastrums) by its more or less up-facing blooms, which are in clusters of a few to 10. These have their 6 petals identical in size and shape, whereas with amaryllises the inner 3 differ somewhat from the outer 3. In the typical species they are glowing scarlet but varieties range from white through salmon-pink to red. The Scarborough-lily, more popular in Europe than America, has large bulbs and broad, nearly strap-shaped evergreen leaves up to 1½ feet or more long. Its flowering stalks are erect, hollow, and 1 to 4 feet tall. The open-trumpet shaped blooms are 3 to 4

67. Scarborough Lily

inches in length by 2½ to 3 inches wide across their faces.

How to grow. Bright sunporch or window in cool room is best. Keep at 50° F. winter nights, to 65° F. days. Growing period: late spring to late fall, during which keep soil evenly moist. In winter let go nearly dry between waterings. In growing period give dilute liquid fertilizer to well-rooted plants every 7 to 10 days. Disturb roots only if absolutely necessary; repot young plants every 2 to 3 years, old ones less often, in June. Between repottings, prick away old soil, replace. Use coarse, fertile, porous soil for potting, top-dressing. Propagate by offset bulbs, or by seed. Seedlings take several years to reach flowering. Vallotas are of the lily family.

68 ❧ Tulips (*Tulipa gesneria*), members of the lily family, are too well known to need detailed description, but few American home gardeners force them indoors. Holland comes to mind when one thinks of tulips. That country is the source of nearly all tulip bulbs sold throughout the world, although that wasn't always so. The first tulip seen by a European was in a garden near Constantinople in 1554. By then tulips had been grown for centuries in Turkey; the Turkish name *tulipan* alludes to their resemblance of the flowers to turbans. When the first tulips arrived in Europe they created a horti-cultural sensation. Tulipomania, one of the wildest speculations the world has ever known, struck Holland in 1634. Fantastic, rapidly soaring prices were paid for bulbs of rare varieties. For one of "Semper Augustus," twelve acres of good building land was offered and refused. Eventually a single bulb sold for more than 100,000 *florins,* a vast fortune. After 3 years the crash came. Countless speculators were bankrupted. But from the wreckage, the capable Hollanders built a bulb industry worth many times the most extravagant value placed on their holdings at the height of the tulipomania.

How to grow. Choose single early or double early varieties. Buy only plump, heavy, top-size bulbs as early in fall as possible. Treat them exactly as advised for hyacinths, but plant more bulbs in each pot, setting them so they nearly touch. Also, don't keep them in the dark after they are brought indoors.

69. Veltheimia

69 ❧ Veltheimias (*Veltheimia*) are South African bulbs of easy culture in sunny windows and sunrooms that are in winter, from the American viewpoint, a little on the cool side. Like many bulb plants from the Southern Hemisphere they go completely dormant in summer. Veltheimias (there are only about 3 sorts, and these differ but little from each other) belong in the lily family and have large, round to somewhat egg-shaped, bulbs, from which sprout several wavy-margined, lance-shaped leaves 6 to 12 inches long, 1 to 3 inches wide. According to kind they are glossy green to waxy and bluish. The flower spikes bring to mind those of certain aloes or of those of red-hot poker plants but are muted pink to soft coral-red. The many drooping flowers overlap to form a dense cylindrical spike at the end of an erect leafless stalk 9 to 18 inches tall. The blooms are tubular, 1 to 1½ inches long.

How to grow. These need 50 to 55° F. winter nights, up to 75° F. days, humidity no less than 40 to 50%. Water copiously when growth starts in fall until foliage dies about May; taper off to nothing as dormancy approaches. Fertilize mildly when in full growth; not enough to encourage lush foliage. In summer store dry in cellar or the like. Repot every few years only, setting bulbs ⅓ above surface. Pack soil firmly. Propagate by offsets, by seeds, by using entire leaves as cuttings.

Numbers 70–81 *are cactuses and other succulents that, to varying degrees according to kind, withstand dry atmospheres much better than most other plants.*

---

70 ❧ The bishop's cap (*Astrophytum myriostigma*) native to Mexico, looks a little like a bishop's miter. It belongs in the cactus family, which—except for possibly one species which may be indigenous to Africa and Asia—occurs natively only in the Americas. It is rare among cactuses because it is without spines. When out of bloom, it appears to be carved out of grayish stone. Basically spherical, 4 to 8 inches across and about as high, it may elongate somewhat with age. It has 5, occasionally 4 or up to 8 strongly developed longitudinal ridges with deep valleys between. Its entire surface is clothed with minute star-shaped hairs or scales, which are responsible for the whiteish-gray coloring. The satiny blooms, borne with considerable freedom in summer and fall, are yellow or yellow with red centers, and are about 2 inches more wide.

How to grow. Few cactuses grow in pure sand—desert soil has lots of mineral nutrients. For potting, use fertile topsoil mixed with enough sand, grit, or perlite to make it very porous; add bonemeal, two heaped teaspoonfuls to the pint; ⅛ part by bulk dried cow manure; compost or leaf mold; unless soil is alkaline, use ⅛ by bulk crushed limestone. Pot firmly, not burying base of plant deeply. Full

70. Bishop's Cap

sun; winter nights at about 55° F.; up to 70° F. days. Soil nearly dry in winter; water moderately, let go quite dryish between waterings, spring to fall. Propagation: very easy by seeds.

71 ❧ Crassulas (*Crassula*) are of numerous sorts. Many, including the delightful miniature "Morgan's Beauty," are excellent house plants. They vary considerably in appearance and size; some are erect and bushy, others are trailers, and some form neat rosettes of foliage. Practically all are succulents, that is have fleshy stems and foliage, and because they predominantly are plants of desert and semideserts, they adapt well to arid atmospheres. The majority are natives of Africa, some occur in other warm parts of the world. Crassulas belong in the orpine family. They have opposite, usually stalkless leaves, those of the pairs often united at their bases. The small, generally five-petaled flowers, white, pink, or sometimes yellowish or greenish, are commonly in clusters, rarely are solitary. The hybrid "Morgan's Beauty," offspring of *C. falcata* and *C. mesembrianthemopsis,* has rosettes of blunt, broadly egg-shaped, thick gray-green leaves and nearly stalkless, rounded clusters of beautiful pink flowers. Other delightful crassulas suitable for window gardens include *C. falcata, C. lactea, C. multicava, C. per-foliata,* and *C. portulacea.*

How to grow. These winter well at 50 to 60° F. nights, to 75° F. days, with full exposure to sun fall to spring, give enough shade to break the fiercest sun of summer. Soil: 2 parts good topsoil, one part sand, grit, or perlite, one part organic matter, with 2 teaspoonfuls bonemeal to a pint of mix. Repot any time, best spring or early summer. Water sparingly November to March, more other times; always let soil go fairly dry before watering. Propagate by cuttings and leaf cuttings in sand, perlite, vermiculite kept barely moist.

72 ❧ The crown-of-thorns (*Euphorbia milii* or *E. splendens*) and related species, such as *E. lophogona* and hybrids with flowers, the showy parts of which are a matched pair of small, rounded to kidney-shaped red, pink, or yellowish bracts, are good window plants. They are members of the spurge family, natives of dry parts of Madagascar. The crown-of-thorns is a very thorny shrub containing abundant milky latex. It has sprawling, branched more or less inter-twined stems and light green reverse-egg-shaped leaves 1 to 3 inches long. The bracts of its flowers are red. From it *E. lophogona* differs in having erect, swollen stems with hair-like fringes instead of thorns. Its leaves are much bigger, its flowers pink. The so-called giant crown-of-thorns is a splendid intermediate hybrid between *E. milii* and *E. lophogona.* The true flowers of all of these are tiny and not showy but are accompanied by colorful, long-lasting bracts ½ to 1 inch more in diameter.

How to grow. If these don't flower, you have given too much shade, failed to keep soil bone-dry. a few weeks each year. They need porous soil, good light, full sun half of each day; ordinary house temperatures, dry air. When in leaf, water regularly; let soil go nearly dry between waterings. When foliage dies, keep soil dry until young leaves appear. Cuttings should be air-dried in shade one week before planting in sand or perlite kept barely moist. Seeds germinate readily.

73 ❧ That *Euphorbia canariensis* is not a cactus but a close relative of the Christmas poinsettia, adapted to a harsh arid environment. In the wild *E. canariensis* must cope with the same high temperatures, intense light, drying winds, and dearth of water that desert cactuses know. The *loss* of mois-ture from its fleshy, leafless stems—which contain sticky, white sap and are enclosed in thick, waxy skin—is reduced to a minimum. The thorns effectively deter browsing animals. Euphorbias are members of the spurge family. As its name suggests, *Euphorbia canariensis* is native of the Canary Islands. Other very similar species inhabit parts of Africa. Flowers are more interesting than showy. The blooms are the equivalents of the tiny yellow ones which, in poinsettias, are encircled by usually brilliant red bracts (leaves)—often quite mistakenly thought to be petals. Plants of *Euphorbia canariensis* are often several years old before they bloom.

73. Euphorbia canariensis

How to grow. Don't kill this with kindness. Let soil go almost completely dry between saturations; be sure pot is well drained, soil porous. One-third by bulk coarse sand or crushed brick, little organic matter. Repot every 3 to 5 years only, big plants less often. Fertilize mildly 2 to 3 times in summer. Full sun or shade with good light, ordinary house temperatures, dry air, suit this plant. Dry cuttings in shade 7 to 14 days before planting in sand or perlite kept barely moist.

74 🌿 Houseleeks or hens-and-chickens (species and hybrids of *Sempervivum*) are hardy outdoor plants in rock gardens, attractive in pots indoors, and almost neglect-proof. The name houseleek alludes to *S. tectorum* often being planted on roofs of cottages in Europe, hens-and-chickens to the clusters of young rosettes of foliage that crowd around

74. Houseleeks

older ones. The botanical name, from the Latin *semper,* ever, and *vivo,* I live, indicates tenacity to life. Planting houseleeks on roofs deferred to the ancient belief that they warded off lightning, and, according to some, fire and sorcery; Charlemagne ordered them to be planted on every house. Houseleeks (there are about 30 natural species and innumerable varieties and hybrids) belong in the orpine family and are natives of Europe and temperate Asia. They have dense rosettes of succulent leaves and erect, fleshy stalks with starry, pink, purple, yellow, or white small flowers.

How to grow. Because they are low, of spreading habit, and don't root deeply, houseleeks look best in shallow flower-pots gardeners call pans. Pots must be well drained; use gritty, not very fertile soil. Grow in full sun. Keep houseleeks cool in winter. Let the soil become dry between waterings. Delay repotting as long as practicable, until rosettes become crowded. Propagate by replanting the usually freely produced offset plants or "chickens."

75 ✿ *Kalanchoe blossfeldiana*—the name is pronounced kal-an-**ko**-ee—and varieties and hybrids of it have become popular in florists' shops largely because their times of blooming are easily controlled by using artificial light or shading to determine the number of hours of darkness the plants receive out of each 24. The species *K. blossfeldiana* is native of Madagascar. Its varieties and hybrids are bushy, branching, succulent plants 6 to 12 inches or more tall. They have slightly toothed elliptic leaves 1 to 2 long and a wealth of

79

75. Kalanchoe

small starry, red, yellow, or orange flowers. Like all kalanchoes, this is a member of the orpine family.

How to grow. Start with a store plant. Cut off flowers after the fade, stand plant in sunny window 65 to 72° F. days, to 55° F. nights, 30% humidity and up. If it is spring or summer, repot soon. If winter, wait until spring. Pot in mix of equal parts, good topsoil, organic matter, and coarse sand or perlite, with *one* teaspoonful bonemeal to each pint of mix. Press soil fairly firmly; let go dryish before each watering. When roots fill pot, give dilute liquid fertilizer until early fall, then stop. To make these flower: keep in complete dark 14 hours a day for 8 weeks; follow with some weeks of somewhat longer days. Natural light, without day-extending artificial light, stimulates spring bloom. Propagate easily by cuttings, leaf cuttings, and seeds.

76 ❧ Moon cactuses (*Selenicereus*), together with *Hylocereus, Nyctocereus,* and some other genera of the cactus family are known collectively as night-blooming cactuses or night-blooming cereuses. They all are remarkable for the size of their amazing blooms that last for but one night. These are big plants that need considerable room. Native to southern Texas, the West Indies, South America, these moon cactuses are not desert plants. They usually perch on trees without taking nourishment from their hosts, like most orchids; they are epiphytes. They have slender, trailing
80

80. Stone Plant (Conophytum frutescens)

80. Stone Plant (Lithops)

81. Easter Cactus

81. Christmas Cactus

82. Browallia Speciosa Major

84. Exacum Affine

86. Dwarf Marigold

87. Patience Plant

93. Firecracker Vine

96. Passionflowers

100. Lily-of-the-Valley

101. Primrose (Primula veris)

101. Primrose (Primula polyanthus)

or climbing, ribbed stems, in the wild often measuring many feet, and with aerial roots. Along the ribs are clusters of short to needlelike spines. Among the biggest and most beautiful in the cactus family, they are usually white with yellow to brownish-yellow outer petals. The sometimes-fragrant flowers are up to a foot long by 10 inches wide. They begin opening about sunset, are magnificent through the night, and start to wither with the coming of dawn.

How to grow. Full sun, perhaps with light shade in summer; 45 to 55° F. winter nights, up to 70° F. days; ordinary house humidity. Pot in spring in coarse, porous, fairly fertile soil; big plants need repotting infrequently. Train stems to stakes or wires. Water moderately spring to fall, occasionally in winter. Give dilute liquid fertilizer twice monthly to well-rooted plants. Cuttings root easily in barely damp sand, perlite, etc.

77. Orchid Cactus

77 ❧ Orchid or leaf cactuses, species and hybrids of *Epiphyllum* of the cactus family, are spectacular bloomers. True cactuses, unrelated to orchids, they are not desert plants, but naturally grow in more humid regions perched on trees. Like orchids, they take no nourishment from their hosts and so are epiphytes. The species range in the wild from Mexico and the West Indies to tropical South America. Though their much-flattened, toothed or scalloped stems greatly resemble leaves, these plants are without true leaves. Their spineless stems function as such. The many-petaled flowers vary from about 2½ to 12 inches in diameter.

Medium-sized sorts average from 4½ to 6½ inches. They come in an immense range of colors and blends, some wonderfully iridescent. Besides white, the hues include creamy-yellows, pinks, lavender-pinks, ambers, rose-pinks, and orchid-pinks, oranges, ambers, coppery tones, purples, reds, and crimsons.

How to grow. These don't like desert conditions. Soil must be slightly acid, half by bulk coarse compost, leaf mold or sphagnum, plus equal parts topsoil and sand, grit, perlite or crushed brick. Add sprinklings cow manure, peanut-sized charcoal. If needed repot in July. Give good light, some shade from strong summer sun, humidity 30% and up. On bright days mist the plant. Keep soil moist except 2 weeks after blooming ends in summer and from November to February; keep drier these times. Winter nights keep at 50° F. Propagate by cuttings in peat moss and sand mix.

78 ❧ The peanut cactus (*Chamaecereus silvestri*) is an endearing miniature, native of Argentina. The only one of its genus, it is attractive for window gardens, dish gardens planted with succulents, and similar uses. It is one of the easiest of the cactus family to grow on its own roots, or it may be grafted on pieces of erect stems of other cactuses to give round-headed little plants with upright "trunks." This plant forms dense clumps of short stems 1½ to 3 inches long and ½ inch in thickness with 6 to 9 (but usually 8) ribs. The stems detach easily, and if the separated pieces remain in contact with soil, they soon take root and become

78. Peanut Cactus

new individuals. Closely set along the ribs are small cushion-like developments called areoles, from each of which sprouts a cluster of 10 to 15 short bristlelike hairs or spines. The glowing scarlet or orange-red flowers are 2 to 3 inches long. There are several excellent hybrids of this cactus, most with less readily detachable stems and bigger blooms.

How to grow. Provide ordinary house temperatures, better low than high, full sun or good light, a little shade from fiercest summer sun. Soil: porous, not infertile; mix good topsoil and grit, perlite or coarse sand; add up to 1/6 by bulk organic matter, and 2 teaspoonfuls bonemeal to each pint of mix. Water moderately, let go almost dry between waterings. Use stems as cuttings. To graft: cut base of stem into wedge, insert in slit cut in top of a section of an upright cereus cactus. Pin or bind in place with string or rubber band. Remove ties in a few weeks when union has taken place.

79. Stapelia nobilis

79 ❧ *Stapelia nobilis*—the "noble starflower," as one highly regarded authority calls it—is among the most remarkable productions of the plant world. A member of a genus of plants called "carrion flowers," because of the disgusting odors of some, this gives no such offense. Its blooms are 5-pointed stars that on occasion attain a foot in diameter, more than 7 or 8 inches. They have bowl-shaped centers and are buff- to ochre-yellow streaked around with 5 parallel cross lines of deep purple-crimson and fringed with soft, purple hairs. Their outsides are purplish. These huge blooms are borne by quite diminutive plants. To the nonbotanical

eye these are cactuslike, although not spiny; they are
actually of the milkweed family. This is a fleshy, leafless succulent. Its velvety, green, angled stems are erect, 4 to 8
inches tall.

How to grow. This South African likes dry air, a sunny
place, a little shade from summer's hottest sun. Keep at 50°
F. winter nights, to 65° F. days; more warmth is wanted other
seasons. Let soil go nearly dry between waterings, especially
in winter. Let cuttings dry in shade a week before planting
in sand, perlite or vermiculite kept just moist. Potting soil:
equal parts sandy topsoil, organic matter, and crushed brick,
with a little bonemeal added.

80 ❧ Stone plants or pebble plants are names applied to
several groups of South African succulents of the mesembry-
anthemum relationship, among them members of the genus
Lithops (Greek *lithos,* stone, and *ops,* appearance). Surely
no plants more closely resemble small stones. Lithops are
inhabitants of deserts and semideserts. They grow in stony
places, often with only the tips of their plant bodies above
ground. Mostly not more than an inch tall, some attain twice
that. Each plan consists of a pair of inverted, more or less
conical, very fleshy, water-storing leaves united for most of
their lengths into a single unit, the top of which is flattish
or roundish, wrinkled or not and plain or marbled green,
gray, brown or purplish. The surprisingly beautiful flowers
resemble daisies, but are constructed very differently. They
are white, yellow, or orange, mostly about an inch in diameter. Lithops are members of the carpetweed family.

How to grow. Easy window plants; need sun, light shade
from high summer sun, dry air. When plants are making
new growth from centers, water moderately, letting soil go
almost dry between times; in winter dormancy keep soil dry.
Soil: very porous; topsoil, much coarse sand, crushed limestone if possible, little organic matter. Set several in shallow
pot, with pebbles resembling them. Propagate easily by seeds,
offsets.

81 ❧ Thanksgiving, Christmas, crab, and Easter cactuses
all respond to much the same conditions and care. They are
members of the cactus family that have been subjects of much
confusion with regard to their botanical names. As now
understood, the three first sorts belong in the genus *Schlumbergera*, although frequently they are cataloged under the
discarded name of *Zygocactus*, and the Easter cactus is

Rhipsalidopsis, instead of *Schlumbergera,* which is sometimes listed. Except that the Easter cactus has very symmetrical short-tubed blooms instead of highly asymmetrical, long-tubed ones, these plants are much alike. All are natives or hybrids of natives of Brazil. They are epiphytes; that is, they perch on trees without taking nourishment from their hosts. The schlumbergeras come in a variety of flower colors from bright magenta-red to crimson, orange-red, pink and nearly white. These cactuses have arching or drooping, branched, flat and rather leaflike, fleshy, jointed stems that function as leaves. The flowers of the schlumbergeras are 1½ to 2½ inches long, those of the Easter cactus much shorter. All are excellent plants for hanging baskets as well as pots.

How to grow. These need extremely porous soil that can be kept moist but not sodden; one with abundance of organic material, some topsoil, with some grit or perlite, crushed charcoal and a little dried cow manure is fine. Pots not too large; repot big plants every few years only. Give good light, shade from strong sun, winter nights at 50 to 55° F., to 70° F. days. Keep soil quite dryish 4 weeks late summer or early fall, again from end of flowering until new growth starts. Propagate in sand or perlite and peat moss at 70° F., and by grafting to other cactuses.

Numbers 82-89 *are annuals or plants usually grown as annuals that are easily raised from seeds and will bloom indoors within a few weeks or months.*

---

82 ❧ *Browallia speciosa* is an excellent bushy flowering plant for indoor light gardens and for sunny windows shaded lightly in summer. As grown indoors, it reaches a foot or less in height, but attains greater size in its native Colombia. A subshrubby perennial best cultivated as an annual, it is propagated afresh each year. It is one of rather few indoor plants —African violets, blue-lilies-of-the-Nile, hyacinths, and *Plumbago cristata* are others—with blue flowers. There is also a white-flowered variety. Browallia belongs to the nightshade family and so is related to potatoes, tomatoes, eggplants, and angel's trumpet, although to the casual observer it looks like none of those. Its leaves are thinnish, egg-shaped, 1½ to 2½ inches long. The flowers, freely produced in good light, have narrow tubes and faces that are five-pointed stars

1½ to 2 inches in diameter. Another species, *B. americana* of tropical America, has numerous ½ inch wide, purple-blue or white blooms. It responds to the same conditions and care as *B. speciosa*.

How to grow. Sow in light, sandy soil at 65 to 70° F. in February or March to get plants for summer bloom; in August or September for winter flowering. Or root cuttings in sand, perlite, etc., at 70° F. Transplant seedlings or cuttings to small pots. When these fill with roots repot, 3 plants to a 5-inch pot. Use porous, fertile soil packed moderately. Keep room above 60° F., humidity 40% and up, soil always moist. When stems are 4 to 5 inches pinch out tips; pinch out tips of branches at 4 to 5 inches also. When final pots are root-filled, give dilute liquid fertilizer every 7 to 10 days.

83 🌿 The cigar flower *(Cuphea platycentra),* which needs little care, is an old-fashioned favorite of window gardeners. Native of Mexico, it is a bushy but not wood plant with slender, branched stems. From 6 to 12 inches tall, it is nearly or quite hairless, has opposite, pointed, egg- to lance-shaped, thin leaves 1 to 2½ inches long. The name "cigar flower" alludes to the appearance of the little blooms. Solitary from the leaf axils, these are about ¾ inch long, slender, and tubular. They are bright red, tipped with a band of a darker hue, with a whitish mouth. The ensemble suggests a tiny cigar. Cupheas belong to the loosestrife family.

How to grow. It is better to raise new plants fairly frequently than to rely on old ones. Many people treat this

as an annual, start fresh plants each spring, and discard them in fall or when they begin to go straggly, which they do if they get too much warmth or shade or part shade. The cigar flower loves sunshine. New plants can be had from cuttings, which, if made from the ends of firm shoots, root easily in humid air when planted in sand, perlite, or vermiculite kept moderately moist, not wet. Put containers of cuttings in good light out of direct sun, where the temperature is about 55 to 70° F. To raise plants from seeds, sow in sandy soil, and sift the top ¼ inch of soil through a sieve as fine as window screening; or sow on milled sphagnum moss. At about 60° F., seeds germinate in a few days. When big enough to handle easily, transplant the seedlings to small pots; do same with cuttings when they have roots ¾-inch long. When small pots are root-filled, repot as growth makes necessary. Any fertile porous soil suits. Keep it moderately moist. When plants are well rooted in biggest pots you want them in, give dilute liquid fertilizer every 7 to 14 days. To induce branching, pinch out tips of shoots occasionally.

84. Exacum affine

84 ❧ *Exacum affine* is a dainty and delightful native of the island of Socotra, off the northeast coast of Africa. It is an annual or biennial, easily raised from seeds, which responds well to window and indoor light garden cultivation and produces over a long season a profuse display of little starry blue—or in one variety, white—blooms. Of compact, bushy habit, 5 to 12 inches tall, this species belongs in the gentian family. It has rather fleshy stems and foliage. Its bright green leaves are glossy, pointed-egg-shaped and a few distinct longitudinal veins. They are an inch or two long. The flowers have 5 petals and a center eye of golden-tipped stamens.

How to grow. Cuttings can be rooted in sand, perlite, etc., at about 70° F., but best depend on seeds. Sow late winter or spring for summer blooming, late summer for winter flowers, in sandy soil about ⅓ by bulk organic matter. Pot seedlings in small pots, later in 4-inch ones, or from start, set 3 in a 4-inch pot. Pot in fertile porous soil kept fairly moist, not wet. When roots fill pots, give dilute liquid fertilizer every 7 to 14 days. Some summer shade good; at other seasons give full sun. Keep at 60° F. up. Pick faded blooms promptly for neatness and to prolong blooming time.

85 ✿ The Madagascar periwinkle (*Catharanthus roseus* or as it is usually cataloged, *Vinca rosea*) is quite distinct from the evergreen, perennial semivining vincas employed as groundcovers and grown indoors chiefly for their foliage. The plan we are discussing is a tender, bushy perennial. Perhaps originally restricted to Madagascar, it is now cosmopolitan in tropical lands and in regions of cold winters is commonly grown as a summer-flowering annual. It revels in heat and sunshine, is fairly tolerant of dryish atmospheres, and so is adaptable as a window plant and for indoor light gardens. It belongs in the dogbane family. About 9 to 18 inches, or a little taller, it has erect stems and somewhat succulent, glossy, opposite, oblongish leaves 1 to 3 inches long and decorated

85. Madagascar Periwinkle

with a white midrib. Freely produced, its upfacing flowers, 1½ inches wide and suggesting the form of phlox, are typically bright rosy-purple, usually with a reddish central eye. There is a good white-flowered variety, one with white flowers with red eyes, and one with light pink flowers.

How to grow. Cuttings in sand, perlite, etc., in humid air at 60 to 70° F. can be used; seeds are used more often. Sow late spring or early spring in sandy soil at 70 to 75° F. When seedlings have second pair of leaves fairly developed, pot separately in small pots. At 3 to 4 inches, pinch out tips to promote branching. Repot as growth requires. They do well in 4- to 5-inch pots. Soil not too rich but porous is best to prevent rot at stem base. Give full sun, about 65° F. winter nights, to 75° F. days, higher in summer. Water moderately; give well-rooted ones dilute liquid fertilizer every 7 to 14 days.

86 ❧ Dwarf marigolds (varieties of *Tagetes*) are among the best "quickie" flowering house plants. They can bloom within a few weeks of sowing seeds, and, in a sunny window or in an indoor light garden, they will make a gay display for several weeks. They can be bloomed at any time of the year but are perhaps most appreciated in fall, winter, and spring. Midwinter flowering is easier with the aid of artificial illumination than with only natural window light. Too well known to require detailed description, these annuals of the daisy family—despite the labels "African" and "French" applied to certain sorts—are as American as corn, squash, peppers, and tomatoes, none of which was known in Europe before the discovery of America. The wild ancestors of modern marigolds are natives of Mexico. From there, seeds were sent to Europe by the early Spaniards. Present-day sorts are available in tremendous variety as a glance at any fairly complete seed catalog will reveal. As house plants, choose dwarf varieties. These come with flowers of various shades and combinations of yellows, oranges, and browns, ferny foliage sets the blooms off to great advantage.

How to grow. Sow seeds at any time, but for best results in late winter or spring or late summer, at 60 to 70° F. or higher. Use sandy, porous soil. When seedlings have their second pair of leaves, transplant individually to small pots. When these are root-filled, repot in bigger ones. Use porous soil of ordinary quality, not too rich in nitrogen. Pack firmly; keep evenly moist. Pinch tips out of stems at 3 to 4 inches to encourage branching. When pots are root-filled, give occasional applications of dilute liquid fertilizer, don't overdo this or rank growth may result. Keep faded flowers picked. Keep at ordinary house temperatures, humidity of 30% or higher.

87 ❧ Patience plants, or patient lucy (*Impatiens*) are known to house plant gardeners in the British Isles as Busy lizzie, presumably in allusion to the frequency and freedom with which their flowers are borne. Our name "patience plant" is less apt. It is a corruption of the botanical name, which means *impatient* and refers to the ripe seed pods, which, when touched, burst explosively to discharge their contents over a wide area. The familiar wild jewelweed, also known as snapweed, or touch-me-not, is an *Impatiens*. These plants are members of the balsam family. Commonly cultivated patience plants are natives and hybrids of natives of the Old World tropics, the most familiar East African. Because one, *Impatiens sultanii,* has had a part in the parentage of some, all are sometimes known as sultanas. They are bushy, succulent-stemmed plants, 6 to 24 inches tall according to variety, with more or less egg-shaped, slightly-toothed leaves 1½ to 3 inches long. The 1- to 2-inch-wide flowers have flat, 5-petaled faces and behind a long, slender spur. They come in a variety of pinks and reds as well as white— less common are yellow, orange, or tangerine.

How to grow. Few house plants are easier; good in windows and indoor light gardens. Bright illumination, light shade from summer sun, ordinary house temperatures, 50% humidity and up, are basic needs. Soil: mix topsoil, generous organic matter, enough coarse sand or perlite to keep it porous. Mix a heaped teaspoonful lime to a pint of mix if soil is acid. Pack moderately firmly. Apply a dilute liquid fertilizer regularly on well-rooted plants. Propagate from seed or from cuttings set in sand, perlite, etc., or even water. Pinch out shoot tips occasionally to stimulate branching.

88 ❧ The sensitive plant (*Mimosa pudica*) is fun, more often grown as a conversation piece and curiosity than for its blooms, but the latter are pretty, and so is the ferny foliage. Few plants are easier to grow and few interest children as much as this. Native of Brazil, the sensitive plant is now widely naturalized elsewhere in warm regions, including the Gulf States. It is a subshrubby, branching perennial, sometimes 1½ feet tall, usually lower. Its long-stalked leaves have many leaflets arranged in feathery patterns. The little

88. Sensitive Plant before touching

Sensitive Plant after touching

pink flowers are crowded in nearly-spherical heads at the ends of long stalks. This plant belongs in the pea family. The astonishing sensitivity of the leaves is most pronounced at temperatures between 75° and 85° F. Below 60° F. and above 140° F., no movement takes place. Within the critical range, any mechanical stimulus on or near the foliage—a touch, a breath of air, a drop of water, or the flame of a lighted match—results in immediate, rapid, and highly visible folding of the leaflets. If the plants are not disturbed further, recovery is fairly rapid but takes considerably longer than the collapse. Young plants are more sensitive than old ones, and repeated irritations over a short period slow the response.

How to grow. Although perennial, best raised from seed each year. Sow late winter or spring in sandy soil at 65 to 70° F. Pot seedlings singly in small pots; when well rooted, repot in 4-inch pots. Use fertile, porous soil, a little on sandy side. Keep reasonably moist. When largest pots which plants are to occupy are root-filled, give dilute liquid fertilizer every 7 to 14 days. Lushest growth is in terrariums, but these also do well in windows in sun or part-day shade and in indoor light gardens.

89. Wishbone Flower

89 ❧ The wishbone flower (*Torenia fournieri*) is delightful for lightly shaded windows and indoor light gardens. To raise it calls for no great skill. Being annuals, the plants die after blooming, but new ones come easily from seeds, bloom within a very few weeks, and remain attractive for a long time. Native of South Vietnam, the wishbone flower belongs in the figwort family. In the Southern United States and other warm parts, it is used outdoors as a substitute for pansies. From 6 to 12 inches tall and much-branched, it has erect, slender stems and toothed, elliptic to egg-shaped leaves 1½ to 2 inches long. The richly colored, velvety flowers, incredibly numerous and in loose terminal spikes or clusters, have inflated, 5-winged calyxes, and a corolla with an upper lip of 2 spreading petals, a lower one of three. The color pattern in the typical species is a flower tube of pale violet-blue with its upper side yellow, the upper lip of the bloom light blue, and the lower one violet-purple with a yellow
92

blotch on its center lobe. A variety has white flowers blotched on the middle lobe of the lower lip with white.

How to grow. Sow late winter or spring in sandy soil, merely pressing seeds into surface. Moisten by immersing pot partway until surface soil is damp. Keep at 65 to 70° F. When big enough to handle, transplant seedlings 1½ inches apart in another pot. When they begin to grow plant 3 together in 5-inch pots. Use fertile topsoil with generous organic matter, enough coarse sand, perlite, etc., to insure porosity. Pinch out tips of plants when they reach 3 inches. Keep soil moist. When pots are root-filled, fertilize mildly. Pick faded blooms promptly to prolong blooming.

Numbers 90-98 *are vines, some permanent, others that are best raised afresh from seeds each year as annuals.*

90. Black-eyed Susan

90 🌿 Black-eyed-susan vine (*Thunbergia alata*) is an easily grown ornamental of cheerful appearance suitable for pots or hanging baskets. It blooms profusely in summer and fall, and, although perennial, is simple to raise from seeds as an annual. Native to tropical Africa, this responsive species belongs in the acanthus family. Black-eyed-susan vine has slender, twining stems 3 to 5 feet long and opposite, more or less triangular-egg-shaped, long-stalked, toothed leaves 1 to 3 inches in length. The flowers, also long-stalked, come singly from the leaf axils. They are tubular, have 5 rounded, spreading petals, are an inch or a little more across. They are bright orange or buff, cream, or white with rich dark purple throats, but sometimes the marking responsible for the colloquial name is missing. Similar *T. gibsonii* of tropical Africa has same uses, needs the same care. It has bigger, orange blooms with a notch in the end of each petal.

How to grow. Sow seeds in spring in sandy soil. When big enough to handle, transplant singly into small pots; repot as growth requires. Or plant 3 to 5 young plants in a hanging basket. Use fertile soil, equal parts of good topsoil, coarse sand or perlite, organic matter; add bonemeal, two teaspoonfuls to the pint of mix. Keep in sunny window or where they get light shade in brightest part of day. Keep soil moist, not constantly soaked. When final pot is root-filled, give dilute liquid fertilizer every two weeks. Keep at least 55° F. nights, to 70° F. days; 40% humidity up. Use wire, string, or trellis supports, or let stems hang from baskets.

91 ❧ The calico flower (*Aristolochia elegans*) is a member—an elegant one, as its scientific name indicates—of the birthwort family. It is a tropical representative of the genus to which the hardy Dutchman's pipe vine belongs, a somewhat more distant cousin of native wild gingers. In bloom our plant is much showier than these. The name "birthwort" for aristolochias reflects a once widely-held belief called the doctrine of signatures. According to this, the forms of their parts are God's indications to man of the healing virtues possessed by plants. Thus, the liver leaf, with vaguely liver-shaped leaves, must be good for curing diseases of the liver. In the flowers of *Aristolochia,* believers saw a representation of a foetus curled in the womb, a clear indication to them of the plant's value as an aid to childbirth. Native to Brazil, the calico flower is a slender-stemmed, evergreen climber, its leaves with broadly heart-shaped blades 2 to 3 inches long. The attractive blooms on pendulous branches are without petals. The showy part is a tubular calyx with a nearly circular saucerlike face about 3 inches across, rich purple-brown on its inside, outside pale yellowish-green with red-purple veins. Unlike those of many aristolochias, the flowers have no ill odor.

How to grow. Sow seeds late winter or spring in sandy soil at 70° F. Transplant seedlings to small pots; repot as

91. Calico Flower

growth requires. Use ordinary, well-drained, fertile soil. Keep in light window with some shade in summer; ordinary house temperatures, 30% humidity and up. Keep soil evenly moist spring to fall, somewhat dried in winter. Give well-rooted plants dilute liquid fertilizer spring to fall. Provide wires, canes, or trellis as supports.

92 ✿ The cup-and-saucer vine (*Cobaea scandens*) is a vigorous, easily grown climber suitable for festooning a window in a cool room or sunroom and for ornamenting porches in summer. Its botanical name commemorates Father Cobo, a Spanish Jesuit of the 17th century, a student of natural history who lived in America for a number of years. Although none but a botanist would be likely to recognize the affinity,

95

Cobaea is a member of the phlox family. Native to Mexico, this vine climbs by tendrils from the ends of its alternate leaves. Each leaf has 2 to 3 pairs of oblongish to egg-shaped leaflets 2 to 4 inches long. Wild specimens attain heights of 10 to 25 feet but examples in pots exhibit more restraint. The flowers, much resembling those of canterbury bells, but long-stalked and solitary rather than short-stalked and in spires, are deeply cup-shaped, about 2 inches long by nearly as wide. Each sits in a "saucer" that is a big leafy calyx. Typically, the blooms are light lavender-violet to greenish-purple but there is a very attractive variety with white flowers.

92. Cup-and-Saucer Vine

How to grow. Although a perennial, best results are had by treating as an annual. Sow seeds late winter or spring in pot of sandy soil at 60 to 70° F. When seedlings have their second leaves transfer singly to small pots or sow 3 seeds in a 5-inch pot; later pull out all but the strongest. Grow young plants in a light window. Keep soil evenly moist. Repot into larger pots as growth requires; stop at 9-inch pot. Provide string or wire support.

93 ❧ The firecracker vine (*Manettia bicolor*) is a pretty, nearly continuous blooming twiner of such neat habit that it is neither too coarse nor big for even small windows or indoor light gardens. Native to Brazil, it belongs to the madder family and so, strange as it may seem, is a relative of gardenias and oranges. Without detailed examination of the floral parts, even a botanist would scarcely suspect that. There are a goodly number of species of *Manettia* but only one other seems to be cultivated. That, *M. inflata* of Paraguay and Uruguay, is scarcely distinguishable from the one here described and is sometimes grown under its name. The firecracker vine has slender, hairless stems and hairless, nearly stalkless, elliptic leaves 1 to 1½ inches long that taper to fine points. The solitary flowers, about ¾ inch long, are bright red, tipped with yellow. Borne on longish stalks from the leaf axils, they are tubular with somewhat swollen bases and are clothed on their outsides with short hairs. At the mouth of the bloom are 5 tiny lobes (petals).

How to grow. Cuttings root readily in spring in humid air at 60 to 70° F. Set in sand, perlite, etc., kept moist in shade from direct sun. When rooted pot 3 together around edge of small pot. When roots fill this repot in larger. Good flowering plants can be had in 4- to 5-inch pots. Use reasonably fertile, porous soil. At 3 to 4 inches tall pinch out tips to induce branching. Give full sun, ordinary house temperature, humidity of 30% up. Give well-rooted plants dilute liquid fertilizer every 14 days. Provide wires, strings, stakes or trellis as support.

94 ❧ German or parlor ivy (*Senecio mikanioides*) is not a true ivy nor is it German. As a member of the daisy family its botanical affinity is with asters, chrysanthemums, and marigolds. It is unrelated to *Hedera*, the genus of the true ivies. South Africa is the homeland of our plant. An old-time favorite, not usually grown primarily as a flowering plant but for its attractive foliage, in encouraging environments it produces blooms of interest and no small ornamental merit. A twining vine, German ivy has slender succulent stems and alternate, fleshy leaves shaped much like those of English ivy. They are roundish in broad outline and have 5 to 7 conspicuous pointed lobes or angles. The little heads of yellow flowers, without petallike florets, have protruding stamens. They are in clusters of many.

How to grow. Best suited to hanging baskets or pots with trellis, wires, etc., for support. Ordinary-to-cool house temperatures, humidity 30% and up. Plant grows without direct sun, needs much sun to flower well. Take cuttings any time, best spring or early summer. Plant in sand, perlite, etc., in humid air at 55 to 70° F. Set rooted cuttings singly in small

94. German Ivy

pots or 3 around edge of slightly larger pot. When recovered from transplanting shock, pinch out tips of shoots to promote branching. Repot soon in bigger container. Use ordinary, well-drained, fertile soil. Water moderately, letting soil go partly dry between waterings. Fertilize well-rooted plants moderately.

95 ❧ The orange-glow or flame vine (*Senecio confusus*) is very satisfactory for moderately cool windows and sun-rooms. Native of Mexico, it belongs, as a glance at its clusters of brilliant orange blooms clearly shows, to the daisy family. In warm, dryish climates such as that of California it is popular for outdoors. Indoors it may be trained on stakes, or trellises or along wires to soften the lines of a window. Or it can be accommodated in hanging baskets. A robust species, under good conditions in the open its stems may become 15 feet long, but in containers they are more restrained. The orange-glow vine has egg-shaped to elliptic, coarsely-toothed leaves, 1 to 4 inches long by approximately half as wide as their lengths. The flower heads (usually called flowers, although, as typifies daisies, each flower comprises many florets), are in loose clusters at the branch ends. From ¾ to 1 inch across, the heads have a central eye or disk of crowded small florets and about 15, spreading, petallike ray florets.

95. Orange-glow or Flame Vine

How to grow. Little skill needed. Give full sun or at most a little part-day shade. House humidity OK if not near a radiator. Pot in spring in fairly fertile, well-drained soil with not too much organic matter; ¼ to ⅓ by bulk is adequate, the rest equal parts topsoil and coarse sand or perlite. Add bonemeal, a heaped teaspoonful to the pint of mix. Keep at 50-55° F. winter nights, to 70° F. days. Water moderately. Fertilize well-rooted plants sparingly. Trim to size and shape after flowering. Propagate by cuttings in sand, perlite or vermiculite.

96 ❧ Passionflowers (*Passiflora*) owe neither their common nor botanical names to the totally unfounded belief that the delicious fruits of some, when in the tropics are eaten out of hand and used to make refreshing drinks, are aphrodisiac. These names stem from the imaginations of Spanish conquistadors who saw in the strange blooms symbols relating to the death of Christ. To them, the circle of 5 sepals and 5 petals represented the 10 apostles (Peter and Judas being absent). The corona of threadlike projections the crown of thorns, the 5 stamens the 5 wounds, the 3 styles the nails, and according to some, the tendrils the scourges used on Jesus. Passionflowers are tendril-climbing vines of the passionflower family, chiefly natives of tropical America including the West Indies. Those cultivated are evergreen. Their leaves may be lobed or not. The showy, large blooms, solitary or in racemes, are blue, purple, red, white, or various combinations of these. Best adapted as a house plant is the hybrid *P. alato-caerulea*. This has fragrant, 4-inch-wide flowers, with sepals white, petals pinkish on their insides, greenish outside, and a purple, bluish, and white corona.

How to grow. These need fair space, do best in sunrooms, and large light windows. Some summer shade is good, but without good light they don't bloom. Keep at 60° F. winter nights, to 75° F. days, much warmer other seasons. Pot in fertile porous soil kept always moist but somewhat drier in winter than other times. Prune to size and repot or top-dress in spring. Spring to fall give dilute liquid fertilizer every 7 to 14 days. Propagate by cuttings in sand, perlite, etc., at 70° F. or higher, and by seeds.

97 ❧ Rosary vine, or string-of-hearts (*Ceropegia woodii*), is a delightful, not-too-rampant vine suitable for windows and indoor light gardens. It succeeds with minimum care and can be accommodated in pots stood on flat surfaces, but is seen to best advantage in hanging containers of rather small size. These may be pots or baskets. Such receptacles permit the stems decorated with pretty leaves and small tubers that are the "beads" of the rosary, to drape themselves most effectively. Native of South Africa, this vine belongs in the milkweed family and—although you would scarcely realize that from a casual inspection—is kin to the noble starflower presented elsewhere in this book. The rosary vine has slender, almost threadlike stems and pairs of fleshy, heart-shaped, rather distantly spaced leaves ¼ to ¾ inch long, and dark, rich green beautifully marbled with silver. The curiously formed flowers cannot be called showy, but they are interesting. They come from the leaf axils, usually in pairs. They are about 1½ inches long and purplish, and are shaped like narrow, bulbous-based, long-necked flasks topped with a canopy of dark purple, hairy spokes that suggest the ribs of an umbrella. The stem tubers are roundish and brown.

How to grow. Don't kill with kindness; water sparingly. Needs are more like those of cactus than those of lusher tropicals. Use soil with more than usual coarse sand, grit, or perlite with some topsoil and organic matter. Give sun all or most of day. Ordinary house temperatures and humidity OK. Propagation by planting stem tubers and by cuttings is practically foolproof.

97. Rosary Vine

98 ✤ Wax plants (*Hoya*) of the milkweed family, are available in several kinds. Common *H. carnosa* like most is a twining, sometimes stem-rooting, evergreen vine. It and some others come in variegated-leaved varieties as well as plain green-leaved sorts. A most beautiful, nearly continuous bloomer, *H. bella* is a nonvining, low shrub with spreading branches and pendant clusters of blooms as exquisite in form and coloring as the loveliest creations of jewelers. This is adapted for hanging baskets. Hoyas, native from eastern Asia to Australia, have opposite leaves—those of *H. carnosa* thick, oblong-egg-shaped, 3 to 4 inches long, those of *H. bella* smaller, thinner, more sharply pointed. The small, starry, 5-lobed, fleshy flowers in clusters have a 5-pointed fleshy crown at their center and, according to kind, are white, pink, purple or combinations of these. In Hawaii those of *H. carnosa* are used in leis.

98. Wax Plants

How to grow. Hoyas aren't demanding, but vining sorts rarely bloom when young. They grow slowly, best in sunny room with light shade in summer. Ordinary house temperatures suit; best if not above 55° F. winter nights. Humidity 30 to 50% OK. Plant cuttings in sand, perlite, etc., in humid air at about 70° F. Repot established plants at roughly 3-year intervals. These flower best in pots smallish for plant size. Use coarse, fertile, fairly loose soil that drains freely. Prune to shape; repot if needed in spring. Water moderately spring to fall, letting soil go nearly dry between soakings; water sparingly in winter, but don't let soil dry out. Fertilize occasionally in summer. After flowers drop, leave spurlike stems that bore them. They will bloom again.

99. Chrysanthemums

99 ❧ Chrysanthemums (*Chrysanthemum morifolium*), once exclusively fall flowers, now appear in florists' stores every day of the year. This miracle reflects the findings of American scientists who discovered that day length (more accurately, the number of hours of darkness experienced in each 24-hour period) correlated with temperature determines why chrysanthemums bloom. By manipulating these, they found, flowers can be had any time. Such shenanigans are beyond the facilities and competences of most home gardeners but it is easy to grow chrysanthemums for fall bloom. Chrysanthemums are members of the daisy family. Modern sorts are the results of centuries of painstaking breeding by oriental, and subsequently occidental, horticulturists from weedy natives to China. The earliest variety cultivated there, in the 5th century A.D., had yellow blooms; the literal translation of "chrysanthemum" is "golden flower." In the 7th century A.D., white- and purple-flowered varieties appeared. Now chrysanthemums come in all colors except blue and in forms ranging from tiny daisylike blooms to immense "footballs" and elegant thread-petaled sorts.

How to grow. (Meaning how to grow pot chrysanthemums for fall bloom.) Depend upon varieties offered by dealers in hardy plants. In May, root cuttings or start with small rooted pieces from old plants. Pot individually in small pots and successively into bigger ones until July. Pinch the tips out of the plants when 4 inches tall and until early August out of all subsequent branches when 6 inches long. Grow outdoors in full sun, with the pots buried to the rims in sand, soil, sawdust, or peat moss. Put a piece of slate or flat stone under each pot to check roots coming through the drainage hole. Water generously. When final pots are filled with roots give dilute liquid fertilizer weekly. Bring into cool sunroom or similar light location before frost. Keep as near 50° F. at night as possible. After blooming cut down and store, with soil barely moist, in a sunny, cool place.

100 ❧ Lilies-of-the-valley (*Convallaria majalis*) are easy to force into bloom indoors. This can be done with purchased plants grown especially for the purpose, called pips, or with clumps dug from the garden. The lily-of-the-valley is not a lily but belongs to the lily family. It occurs natively in woodlands in northern Europe and Asia and in mountains from Virginia to South Carolina. It has masses of underground stems and roots. In early spring, twin-leaved shoots sprout from the base of each an elegant, slightly arching stalk develops, bearing along one side few to many charming, nodding, deliciously fragrant, white cup-shaped flowers up to nearly ½ inch across. The elliptic leaves are 4 to 8 inches long, up to 3 inches wide.

How to grow. Whether you buy pips or dig plants from the garden, they can only be forced once. After flowering, they are useless for blooming again inside, but if you keep them growing until danger of freezing is passed and then plant them outdoors in a shaded place in dampish, woodland-type soil, they will recover and flower in future years. Plant pips as soon as you receive them, 1½ to 2 inches apart in 4 or 5 inch pots, using sandy soil, or a mixture of sand and peat moss or phagnum moss, or similar material. If necessary, shorten the roots to do this. Set pips with buds just above surface. Keep moist and completely dark at 60 to 70° F. for 10 days; then bring into light. Until foliage greens, shade from sun. In 3 to 4 weeks plants will bloom. As for clumps of home-grown roots, dig these in early fall. Pot in ordinary soil, then bury to rims of pots outdoors in loose material such as compost, peat moss, or sawdust. Keep watered. From January to February, bring indoors, and treat as advised for purchased pips.

101 ❧ Primrose is a collective name for all the many members of the genus *Primula.* Some, notably *P. malacoides* and *P. obconica* with pink, red, and white blooms, are sold by florists as spring-flowering pot plants, although less commonly than formerly. These are annuals, to be discarded after they are through blooming. All you can do is keep them in good condition as long as possible. But there are perennial sorts that can bloom at home, and after flowering, can be planted in the garden to bloom again in future years. Primroses belong in the primrose family and are natives of cool parts of the northern hemisphere. They have rosettes of usually toothed, spoon-shaped to rounded, generally hairy and leafless stalks with a terminal cluster (or several tiered clusters) of white, pink, red, yellow, or orange-colored blooms. They are lovers of cool, moist areas containing abundant organic matter, and shade from strong sun. The florists' sorts are natives of China. Keep them in a bright window without strong sun in a cool room where they won't freeze (40 to 50° F. nights). Keep the soil always decidedly moist. It is a good plan to keep a saucer filled with water under each pot.

How to grow. The best kinds are the English primrose (*P. vulgaris*) and polyanthus primrose (*P. polyanthus*). The first has one flower on a stem, the other a cluster. Blossoms are yellow, orange-yellow, creamy-white, and shades of red and blue. Plants are available from nurseries and garden centers in spring. It is simpler to buy them than to raise from seeds. Plant outdoors in rich soil containing organic matter, in cool, shady spot. Keep well watered. Pick off dead blooms to prevent seeds from forming. In early fall, transplant to pots. Sink to rims outdoors in soil, sand, or peat moss. When ground freezes cover with straw or branches of evergreens. In February bring into a light window in a cool room and water generously. After freezing weather is ended, replant in the garden.

Vocabulary

Bonemeal. A slow-acting fertilizer that supplies some nitrogen and a considerable amount of phosphorus. Consisting of finely ground bones, is used for mixing with potting soil. The nutrients in steamed bonemeal are more readily available than those of raw bonemeal.

Bract. A leaflike organ associated with flowers. Bracts may be green or, like those of poinsettias, colored and petallike.

Compost. This consists of leaves and other vegetation that has been piled and allowed to rot until it has lost most of its original structure; it is a rich, dark brown material, nourishing and encouraging to the growth of roots.

Cuttings. Pieces of stems, or—in the case of leaf cuttings—single leaves or parts of leaves that in suitable environments put down roots and develop into new plants. Except with succulents, which need drier conditions, rooting is encouraged by a little extra warmth, a humid atmosphere, and shade from direct sun.

Dilute liquid fertilizer. Any fertilizer prepared and sold for house plants; as used in this book, it means dilution according to the manufacturer's directions or, better still, to a somewhat greater degree.

Dormant. When plants are without foliage and resting, without any growth activity, they are said to be dormant. Some plants go into a semidormant condition at times.

Grafting. This is a sophisticated method of propagation, rarely attempted by amateurs, whereby a rootless portion of one plant (the scion) is caused to unite with another rooted plant (the understock).

Grit. This consists of tiny fragments of rock somewhat larger than grains of coarse sand.

Hybrid. A plant the parentage of which includes more than

106

one species is called a hybrid. Hybrid plants are often superior horticulturally to the species from which they are derived.

Indoor light gardens. Also called artificial light gardens. These are set-ups designed to permit the cultivation of plants indoors chiefly or entirely by the use of artificial light as a substitute for daylight. Chief dependence is upon fluorescent light, sometimes supplemented with a small amount from ordinary incandescent bulbs.

Inflorescence. This is the botanical term for the natural grouping of flowers as they are displayed on the plant.

Leaf axil. The angle between a leaf and the stem that bears it.

Leaf mold. This is very choice compost made from the leaves of (usually) nonevergreen trees. It is at its best when flaky.

Milled sphagnum moss. Sphagnum is a type of moss that grows in bogs. When dried and ground fine, it is sold as milled sphagnum moss.

Offset. A small bulb, tuber, or plant that grows beside a larger one. Offsets are often used as a means of propagation.

Organic matter or *material.* Anything alive or that has lived is organic. As used by gardeners these terms apply to compost, leaf mold, peat moss and like substances, which as they decay, add humus to the soil.

Osmunda fiber. The roots of osmunda ferns. A wiry material used as a rooting medium for orchids and other plants that in the wild perch on trees (as epiphytes).

Peat moss. This brown organic material consists of dried, partly decayed bog mosses, chiefly sphagnum.

Perlite. An admirable substitute for sand, perlite is a much lighter pulverized volcanic rock. Its particles are porous.

Pinch. This means to nip out the end, the extreme growing point of a shoot, with finger and thumb.

Pots. Containers especially made to grow plants in. Traditionally unglazed clay pots have found most favor, but pots of plastic and of glazed earthware are also used.

Sand. For mixing with potting soil sand should be free of all fine, silty particles. Don't use sea sand unless it has been repeatedly washed to free it of all salts.

Species. · All the individuals of a natural population of plants that are so alike that they can be conceived of as the offspring of a single individual constitutes a species. Thus all plants of the kaffir belong to the species *Clivia miniata.* Within that species may be *varieties* that exhibit minor variations.

Terrarium. A terrarium is a glass- or plastic-sided container resembling an aquarium but with its top enclosed with glass or plastic. In it plants are grown either in pots or planted in a bed of soil. Its great advantage is that it protects from drafts and assures a humid atmosphere around the plants.

Topsoil. Natural soil taken from the upper few inches and congenial to the growth of plants is called topsoil. It is normally much more fertile than deeper layers which are called subsoil.

Tubers. These are bulblike, swollen portions of roots or stems (usually underground) that serve as food-storage organs for some plants. Potatoes are one kind of tuber.

Variety. A variety is a lesser division of a species or hybrid. Thus there are many varieties of common geranium, differing in type of flower foliage, flower color, and other details.

Vermiculite. This consists of particles of mica rock expanded by heat treatment so that each is like a tiny sponge. Unlike particles of perlite, these crush and become compacted under the influence of pressure or weight.

Well-drained soil. Earth so porous that water passes freely through it and allows air to enter is said to be well-drained. In order to maintain this condition it is necessary to have a drainage hole in the bottom of the container.

Well-rooted. A well-rooted plant, as the term is used in this book, refers to one that has filled all or most of its available soil with healthy roots on the extent that when the plant is taken from the pots the roots show as a fairly dense network over the entire plant ball.

Mail-Order Sources *for plants and seeds of flowering house plants. Catalogs are free except as noted.*

Alberts & Merkel, Inc.
Boynton Beach, Florida 33435
Catalog 50¢

Buell's Greenhouses
Eastford, Connecticut 06242
Catalog 25¢
Enclose business-size,
stamped self-addressed envelope

Cactus by Mueller
10411 Rosedale Highway
Bakersfield, California 93307

Desert Plant Company
Box 880
Marfa, Texas 79843

L. Easterbrook Greenhouses
10 Craig Street
Butler, Ohio 44822
Catalog $1

Greenland Flower Shop
Port Matilda, Pennsylvania 10870

Harborcrest Nurseries
1425 Benvenuto Avenue
Victoria, B. C., Canada

Henrietta's Nursery
1345 North Brawley Avenue
Fresno, California 93705
Catalog 25¢

Holmes Bromeliad Nursery
19396 S. W. 248 Street
Homestead, Florida 33612

The House Plant Corner
Oxford, Maryland 21654

Howe Hill Herbs
Camden, Maine 04843

J & L Orchids
20 Sherwood Road
Easton, Connecticut 06812

Lauray of Salisbury
Undermountain Road
Salisbury, Connecticut 06068
Catalog 50¢

Logee's Greenhouses
Danielson, Connecticut 06239
Catalog $1

Lyndon Lyon
14 Mutchler Street
Dolgeville, New York 13329

Merry Gardens
Camden, Maine 04843

New Mexico Cactus Research
P. O. Box 787
Belen, New Mexico 87002

Norvell Greenhouses
318 Greenacres Road
Greenacres, Washington 99016

Geo. W. Park Seed Company
Greenwood, South Carolina 29647

The Plant Room
6373 Trafalgar Road
Hornby, Ontario, Canada

Tropical Paradise Greenhouse
8825 West 79th Street
Overland Park, Kansas 66204

Wilson Brothers
Roachdale, Indiana 46172

INDEX